FLOWERS
their Spiritual Significance

Introduction

What are flowers? Are they not messengers of love, prayers of the vegetal world, the aspiration and adoration of Nature, the smile of the Divine?

Says Sri Aurobindo in his epic poem, Savitri:
"The world's senseless beauty mirrors God's delight.
That rapture's smile is secret everywhere;
It flows in the wind's breath, in the tree's sap,
Its hued magnificence blooms in leaves and flowers."

Flowers may appear frail and fleeting, but for a brief moment they bring a touch of eternity, of joy and beauty which lie beyond the sorrows and cares of the human world. In the beautiful words of Sri Aurobindo,
"Earth's flowers spring up and laugh at time and death."

In all countries flowers have been associated with religion and worship, with myths and legends. And to people all over the world they have been symbols of love and remembrance. A flower contains all the elements of Nature – air, water, fire, earth and ether. Apart from its beauty of form, colour, fragrance and texture there is something more – an indefinable, subtle and mysterious quality about it. In the words of Liselle Raymond, "in its simplicity, it carries the vibrations of the Akasha, *the ethereal element itself, – that is all that is most abstract, pure and perfect. It is, above everything else, the* form, *behind which is the* sound, *the all powerful creative* Mantra.*"*

This is why flowers have charmed and attracted men and women alike, down the ages. It is this subtle element, their soul which has given them a very special place in the life of men and of communities. This is very evident in the Sri Aurobindo Ashram at Pondicherry, where the Mother has revealed the spiritual meaning of flowers, where the flowers are tended with great love, affection and care and are looked upon as powerful means of finding oneself and communing with the Divine.

This book primarily focuses its attention on this new, and not so commonly known, spiritual and deeper aspect of flowers. The flowers have been grouped together according to certain themes in various chapters. The book also takes in its ambit articles from different lands which reveal the many facets of one of the most wonderful of Nature's creations. We begin to see the great truth contained in the lines of Tennyson,
"Little flower – but if I could understand
What you are, root and all, and all in all,
I should know what God and man is."

Yes, if only we could understand or, rather, if only we could be like a flower. Indeed this, in a way, is the entire theme of the book. If it can help to kindle this aspiration in even a few of us, the book will have served its purpose.

Of all the messages sent through flowers, the one which is predominant is love. May we pray with the Mother,
"O Lord, let this pure flower of love blossom in me, so that it may make fragrant all who approach me and its perfume sanctify them."

*Life must blossom like a flower
 offering itself to the Divine.*

　　　　　　　　　　　　　The Mother

Be like a Flower

Be like a flower. One must try to become like a flower: open, frank, equal, generous and kind. Do you know what it means?

A flower is open to all that surrounds it: Nature, light, the rays of the sun, the wind, etc. It exerts a spontaneous influence on all that is around it. It radiates a joy and a beauty.

It is frank: it hides nothing of its beauty, and lets it flow frankly out of itself. What is within, what is in its depths, it lets it come out so that everyone can see it.

It is equal: it has no preference. Everyone can enjoy its beauty and its perfume, without rivalry. It is equal and the same for everybody. There is no difference, or anything whatsoever.

Then generous: without reserve or restriction, how it gives the mysterious beauty and the very own perfume of Nature. It sacrifices itself entirely for our pleasure, even its life it sacrifices to express this beauty and the secret of the things gathered within itself.

And then, kind: it has such a tenderness, it is so sweet, so close to us, so loving. Its presence fills us with joy. It is always cheerful and happy.

Happy is he who can exchange his qualities with the real qualities of the flowers. Try to cultivate in yourself their refined qualities.

THE MOTHER

Soul of a Flower

Have you ever gone into a garden early in the morning? The flowers are facing the sun, awaiting its advent. Have you felt the mighty aspiration that surges all around for the coming light?

Have you watched a bud, completely closed, and how slowly, miraculously, the petals open, one by one? Whence came this force, this energy, this pulsating life?

Have you seen the earth after it has received a few drops of rain? Multi-coloured little hands come out from the earth in a gesture of thanksgiving. They are the fairy-lilies named 'Prayer' by the Mother. We can palpably feel the vibration of gratitude and we look in joy at this spontaneous and beautiful response of Nature. Nature, so receptive, so open to the Grace! If only we could be likewise....

And then we wonder: What is it that gives to a flower, and so often to a child, its beauty, its sweetness, its feeling of a happy self-giving? It is the presence of the Divine in the flowers, in Nature. It is what we call the 'Psychic Presence'. And love.

Love of flowers can help us to find our own psychic being, the Divine within us.

The unselfish movement, uncalculating, is one of the most beautiful forms of psychic consciousness in the world. But the higher one rises in the scale of mental activity, the rarer it becomes. For with intelligence come all the skill and cleverness, and corruption, calculation. For instance, when a rose blossoms it does so spontaneously, for the joy of being beautiful, smelling sweet, expressing all its joy of living, and it does not calculate, it has nothing to gain out of it: it does so spontaneously, in the joy of being and living. Take a human being, well, apart from a very few exceptions, the moment his mind is active he tries to get some advantage out of his beauty and cleverness; he wants it to bring him something, either men's admiration or even much more sordid gains yet. Consequently, from the psychic point of view, the rose is better than human beings.

Only, if you climb a rung higher and consciously do what the rose does unconsciously, then it is much more beautiful. But it must be the same thing: a spontaneous flowering of beauty, uncalculating, simply for the joy of being. Little children have this at times (at times, not always). Unfortunately, under the influence of their parents and the environment, they learn to be calculating when yet very young.

But this kind of wish to gain by what one has or does is truly one of the ugliest things in the world. And it is one of the most widespread, and it has become so widespread that it is almost spontaneous in man. Nothing can turn its back on the divine love more totally than that, that wish to calculate and profit.

Do flowers love?

This is their form of love, this blossoming. Certainly, when one sees a rose opening to the sun, it is like a need to give its beauty. Only, for us, it is almost unintelligible, for they do not think about what they do. A human being always associates with everything he does this ability to see himself doing it, that is, to think about himself, think of himself doing it. Man knows that he is doing something.

Animals don't think. It is not at all the same form of love. And flowers, so to speak, are not conscious: it is a spontaneous movement, not a consciousness that is conscious of itself, not at all. But it is a great Force which acts through all that, the great universal Consciousness and the great Force of universal love which makes all things blossom in beauty.

*

Is there a sense of beauty in flowers?

Directly there is organic life, the vital element comes in, and it is this vital element which gives to flowers the sense of beauty. It is not perhaps individualised in the sense we understand it, but it is a sense of the species and the species always tries to realise it. I have noticed a first rudiment of the psychic presence and vibration in vegetal life, and truly this blossoming one calls a flower is the first manifestation of the psychic presence. The psychic is individualised only in man, but it was there before him; but it is not the same kind of individualisation as in man, it is more fluid: it manifests as force, as consciousness rather than as individuality. Take the rose, for example; its great perfection of form, colour, scent expresses an aspiration and a psychic giving. Look at a rose opening in the morning at the first touch of the sun, it is a magnificent self-giving in aspiration.

*

What is this psychic prayer that flowers represent?

The psychic, when it manifests in a plant, in the form of a flower, is in the form of a wordless prayer; it is the élan of the plant towards the Divine.

*

You have written: "Love of flowers is a valuable help for finding and uniting with the psychic." Could you explain this more in detail?

Since flowers are the manifestation of the psychic in the vegetal kingdom, love of flowers would mean that one is drawn by the psychic vibration and consequently by the psychic in one's own self.

When you are receptive to the psychic vibration, that puts you in a more intimate contact with the psychic in your own self. Perhaps the beauty of flowers too is a means used by Nature to awaken in human beings the attraction for the psychic.

How can one enter into psychic contact with flowers?

When one is in conscious contact with one's own psychic, one becomes aware of an impersonal psychic behind the whole creation and then, through this, one can enter into contact with flowers and know the psychic prayer they represent.

THE MOTHER

Prayer
Self-giving is true prayer.

Flowers – their Spiritual Names

Flowers are the 'wordless prayers of Nature', beautiful expressions of its yearning for the Divine. And each flower has its unique aspiration, its own vibration, its true meaning.

Very rarely do the botanical or the common names given to flowers represent their true meaning. The Mother has given spiritual names to nearly eight hundred flowers revealing their deepest aspiration. She has also described the process, though it is not something which can be done by the mind. In several cases, the name given by the Mother is very much in harmony with the common name given traditionally or the use to which a flower is put, specially in worship.

The lotus, the flower of the gods, is named by the Mother the Avatar or the Divine Consciousness. Tulsi is an inseparable part of all worship in India and is offered to Vishnu and Krishna. The name given by the Mother to Tulsi is 'Devotion'. Shiva, the eternal ascetic, is offered the wild Dhatura flower which the Mother called 'Tapasya' meaning askesis. Kali, the mighty Goddess of strength, is worshipped with the red hibiscus named 'Power' by the Mother. And then we have the Mudar, named 'Courage' by the Mother, which is offered to Hanuman, the courageous and devoted servitor of the Divine. The Sunflower, forever facing the sun, is 'Consciousness turned towards the Divine'. And what about those unforgettable tiny flowers popularly known as 'Forget-Me-Not'? To these, the Mother has given the name of 'Lasting Remembrance'. The bright orange flower of the tree called 'Ashoka' in India, under whose spreading branches captive Sita sat in Lanka, means in Sanskrit exactly what the Mother has called it, 'Without Grief'.

There are other flowers whose significance, as given by the Mother, has reference to the name of a god or goddess. In particular there are several flowers named after Krishna. Most of these flowers are blue, the colour associated with Krishna and, in the Water Hyacinth called by the Mother 'Krishna's play in the Vital', one can even see the peacock plume.

Mother, when flowers are brought to you, how do you give them a significance?

To the flowers? But it's in the same way, by entering into contact with the nature of the flower, its inner truth. Then one knows what it represents.

*

Tapasya
*A discipline aiming at
the realisation of the Divine.*

Each flower has its special significance, hasn't it?

Not as we understand it mentally. There is a mental projection when one gives a precise meaning to a flower. It may answer, vibrate to the touch of this projection, accept the meaning, but a flower has no equivalent of the mental consciousness. In the vegetable kingdom there is a beginning of the psychic, but there is no beginning of the mental consciousness. In animals it is different; mental life begins to form and for them things have a meaning. But in flowers it is rather like the movement of a little baby – it is neither a sensation nor a feeling, but something of both; it is a spontaneous movement, a very special vibration. So, if one is in contact with it, if one feels it, one gets an impression which may be translated by a thought. That is how I have given a meaning to flowers and plants – there is a kind of identification with the vibration, a perception of the quality it represents and, little by little, through a kind of approximation (sometimes this comes suddenly, occasionally it takes time), there is a coming together of these vibrations (which are of a vital-emotional order) and the vibration of the mental thought, and if there is a sufficient harmony, one has a direct perception of what the plant may signify.

In some countries (particularly here) certain plants are used as the media for worship, offering, devotion. Certain plants are given on special occasions. And I have often seen that this identification was quite in keeping with the nature of the plant, because spontaneously, without knowing anything, I happened to give the same meaning as that given in religious ceremonies. The vibration was really there in the flower itself….Did it come from the use that had been made of it or did it come from very far, from somewhere deep down, from a beginning of the psychic life? It would be difficult to say.

If our flower-offering depends on our state of consciousness, does it help us to learn the significances of flowers even if it is purely mental to begin with?

Yes, surely.

THE MOTHER

Krishna's play in the Vital
It is in His midst that it has all its charm

Flowers where the spiritual name matches perfectly with the common name or with the way the flowers are used traditionally.

No.	Spiritual Name	Common Name (India)	Common Name (West)	Botanical Name	Explanation
1.	Devotion	Tulsi		Ocimum sanctum	Very sacred plant in India used for worship since ancient times
2.	Dynamic Power	Java	Hibiscus	Hibiscus	Offered to Kali the Goddess of power and strength
3.	Tapasya	Dhatura	Angel's Trumpet	Datura suaveolens	Offered to Shiva the Lord of ascetics
4.	Devotional attitude	Bael	Wood apple	Aegle marmelos	Leaves and flowers offered to Shiva
5.	Courage	Mudar		Calotropis procera	Offered to Hanuman the courageous and devoted servitor of the Divine
6.	Without Grief	Ashoka		Saraca Indica	The spiritual name matches perfectly with the popular name in India
7.	Lasting remembrance		Forget me not	Myosotis	The spiritual name matches perfectly with the popular name in the West
8.	Consciousness turned towards the Light	Suryamukhi	Sunflower	Helianthus	This flower always turns its face to the sun

Flowers whose spiritual significance has reference to the name of gods or goddesses.

No.	Spiritual Name	Common Name (India)	Common Name (West)	Botanical Name
1.	Satchidananda	Dulaba Champa	Ginger lily	Hedychium
2.	Godhead		Hibiscus Hawaian	Hibiscus 'Hawaian'
3.	Integral Wealth of Mahalakshmi		Water Lily	Nymphaea
4.	Mahasaraswati's Perfection in works		Sweet-smelling Rondeletia	Rondeletia odorata
5.	Aditi – The Divine Consciousness	Safed Kamal	White Lotus	Nelumbo nucifera 'Alba'
6.	The Avatar – The Supreme manifested on earth in a body	Lal Kamal	Red Sacred Lotus	Nelumbo Nucifera
7.	Krishna's light in the Overmind		Blue Sage	Salvia farinacea
8.	Krishna's ananda		Cape leadwort	Plumbago auriculata
9.	Krishna's integral play		Wishbone flower	Torenia fournieri 'Alba'
10.	Krishna's light in the mind	Mulata	Heavenly Blue	Thunbergia grandiflora
11.	Krishna's light in the physical mind			Ruellia ciliosa
12.	Krishna's light in the vital			Ruellia tuberosa
13.	Krishna's play in the vital		Water Hyacinth	Eichhornea crassipes
14.	Krishna's light in the senses		Butterfly pea	Clitoria ternatea
15.	First sign of Krishna's light in matter			Evolvulus alsinoides
16.	Krishna's play in matter			Torenia fournieri
17.	Krishna's light in the subconscient			Eranthemum wattii
18.	Krishna's influence in the subconscient	Priya-darsa	Crossandra	Crossandra
19.	Radha's consciousness (ultramarine)	Aparajita		Clitoria ternatea
20.	Radha's consciousness in the vital (light purple)			Clitoria ternatea
21.	Protection of the gods	Baganvilas	Bougainvillea	Bougainvillea

Flowers containing Sri Aurobindo's name.

1.	Sri Aurobindo's compassion		Rose Moss	Portulaca grandiflora
2.	Remembrance of Sri Aurobindo			Lobelia erinus
3.	Opening to Sri Aurobindo's Force			Thunbergia kirkii
4.	The Avatar –The Supreme manifested on earth in a body	Lal Kamal	Red sacred lotus	Nelumbo nucifera

Flowers around us

There are some flowers with which we are all familiar, which are known as common flowers. But with the spiritual meaning given to them by the Mother, they appear to us revealed in a new light, with an added significance. Jasmine is 'Purity', and the Bougainvillea, planted all around the house, is 'Protection'. The Chrysanthemum is 'Life Energy', and the Pansy is 'Thoughts turned towards the Divine'. The Gulmohar is 'Realisation', the Sadabahar blooming throughout the year is 'Progress', Gladioli is 'Receptivity' and the Marigold, 'Plasticity'.

Consciousness turned towards the Supramental Light
It is athirst for Truth and will find its satisfaction only in the Truth.

Plasticity
*Always ready for the
progress demanded.*

Progress
The reason why we are on earth.

*To see the world in a grain of sand,
And heaven in a wild flower,
Hold infinity in the palm of your hand,
And eternity in an hour.*

William Blake

Obedience
*To learn to obey is good;
to obey only the Divine is better.*

Life Energy
Powerful and manifold, it meets all needs.

Some well known and common flowers.

No	Spiritual Name	Common Name (India)	Common Name (West)	Botanical Name
1.	Aristocracy of Beauty		Iris	Iris
2.	Aspiration	Parijata	Night Jasmine	Nyctanthes arbor-tristis
3.	Attachment for the Divine		Orchid	Orchidaceae
4.	The Avatar – The Supreme manifested on earth in a body	Lal Kamal	Red sacred lotus	Nelumbo nucifera
5.	Balance		Begonia	Begonia
6.	Beginning of the Supramental Realisation	Palash	Flame of the Forest	Butea monosperma
7.	Beauty in Art	Udsalep	Peony	Paeonia
8.	Bird of Paradise		Tiger-claw Plant	Heliconia metallica
9.	Blossoming		Tulip	Tulipa
10.	Boldness		Cockscomb	Celosia argentea cristata
11.	Collaboration		Carnation	Dianthus caryophyllus
12.	Complexity of the Centres		Canna	Canna
13.	Consciousness turned towards the Light	Suryamukhi	Sunflower	Helianthus
14.	Constant Remembrance of the Divine		Japanese Honeysuckle	Lonicera Japonica
15.	Courage	Mudar		Calotropis procera
16.	Distincion		Lilac	Syringa
17.	Dynamic Power	Java	Hibiscus	Hibiscus

To me the meanest flower that blows can give
Thoughts that do often lie too deep for tears.
                                    William Wordsworth

No.	Spiritual Name	Common Name (India)	Common Name (West)	Botanical Name
18.	Endurance		Zinnia	Zinnia
19.	Enthusiasm		Petunia	Petunia hybrida
20.	Gentleness		Sweet Pea	Lathyrus odoratus
21.	Integral Purity	Mogra	Jasmine	Jasminum
22.	Joy of Vegetal Nature in answer to the New Light		Bottle Brush	Callistemon
23.	Lasting Remembrance		Forget-me-not	Myosotis
24.	Life Energy	Chandramallika	Chrysanthemum	Chrysanthemum morifolium
25.	Love for the Divine	Gulab	Rose	Rosa
26.	Modesty		Sweet Violet	Viola odorata
27.	Nature makes an offering of her beauty		Morning Glory	Ipomoea
28.	The New Creation	Rajnigandha	Tuberose	Polianthes tuberosa
29.	Nobility		Dahlia	Dahlia
30.	Plasticity	Genda	Marigold	Tagetes
31.	Power of Beauty		Daffodil	Narcissus
32.	Progress	Sadabahar		Vinca roseus
33.	Protection	Baganvilas	Bougainvillea	Bougainvillea
34.	Psychological Perfection	Champaka	Temple Tree	Plumeria
35.	Realisation	Gul Mohar	Flamboyant	Delonix regia
36.	Receptivity		Gladiolus	Gladiolus
37.	Riches		Cactus Flower	Cactus
38.	Spiritual Atmosphere	Neem	Margosa	Azadirachta indica
39.	Spiritual Happiness		Garden Geranium	Pelargonium hortorum
40.	Spontaneous Joy of Nature		Poppy	Papaver rhoeas
41.	Supramental Influence in the Subconscient	Priyadarsha	Crossandra	Crossandra
42.	Supramental Psychological Perfection	Champak	Golden Champa	Michelia champaca
43.	Supramental Sun	Kadamba		Anthocephalus indicus
44.	Surrender	Gulab	Country Rose	Rosa
45.	Thoughts turned towards the Divine		Pansy	Viola tricolor hortensin
46.	Transparency		Aster	Callistephus chinensis
47.	Wealth		Water Lily	Nymphaea
48.	Without Grief	Ashoka	Sorrowless Tree of India	Saraca indica

Silent Language of Flowers

Flowers have always been an intrinsic part of life in the Ashram. For several years, the Mother distributed flowers to the sadhaks every day. This is not merely because of the love of beauty which pervades the Ashram atmosphere, nor is it because flowers are a part of worship in all countries. In the words of Sahana Devi, "there (at the Ashram) it is much more, it has been the language of our inner communication with the Mother. How often have we not intimated our heart's yearnings through the flowers and received her blessings and directions through them." Adds Lizelle Raymond, "the one who receives a flower from her hands knows that it is a living Mantra, *which will act profoundly in its time; all depends on the opening, on the sincerity, on the surrender of the one who delivers himself to the Divine influence. There is here a process of transmutation, of stimulation, which is evident. The flower is the active agent which accomplishes the aim... The mute message of the flower is neat, precise, often as sharp as a razor's edge... At the very moment he receives the flowers they become for him literally the steps of the stairs of light he has to climb."*

Q. What is the significance of the Mother's giving us flowers at Pranam every day?

A. It is meant to help the realisation of the thing the flower stands for.

*

Q. Are flowers mere symbols and nothing more? Can the flower symbolising silence, for example, help in the realisation of silence?

A. It is when the Mother puts her force into the flower that it becomes more than a symbol. It then can become very effective if there is receptivity in the one who receives.

SRI AUROBINDO

*

I can transmit a state of consciousness more easily to a flower than to a man: it is very receptive, though it does not know how to formulate its experience to itself because it lacks a mind. But the pure psychic consciousness is instinctive to it. When, therefore, you offer flowers to me their condition is almost always an index to yours. There are persons who never succeed in bringing a fresh flower to me – even if the flower is fresh it becomes limp in their hands. Others, however, always bring fresh flowers and even revitalise drooping ones. If your aspiration is strong your flower-offerings will be fresh. And if you are receptive you will be also very easily able to absorb the message I put in the flowers I give you. When I give them, I give you states of consciousness; the flowers are the mediums and it all depends on your receptivity whether they are effective or not.

*

When I give flowers, it is as an answer to the aspiration coming from the very depths of your being. It is a need or an aspiration, it depends upon the person. It may fill a void or else give you the impetus to progress, or it may help you find the inner harmony in order to establish peace.

The Mother in Japan in 1919

*

Flowers are extremely receptive. All the flowers to which I have given a significance receive exactly the force I put into them and transmit it. People don't always receive it because most of the time they are less receptive than the flowers, and they waste the force that has been put in it through their unconsciousness and lack of receptivity. But the force is there, and the flower receives it wonderfully.

I knew this a very long time ago. Fifty years ago…. There was that occultist who later gave me lessons in occultism for two years. His wife was a wonderful clairvoyant and had an absolutely remarkable capacity – precisely – of transmitting forces. They lived in Tlemcen. I was in Paris. I used to correspond with them. I had not yet met them at all. And then, one day, she sent me in a letter petals of the pomegranate flower, "Divine Love". At that time I had not given the meaning to the flower. She sent me petals of pomegranate flowers telling me that these petals were bringing me her protection and force.

Now, at that time I used to wear my watch on a chain. Wrist-watches were not known then or there were very few. And there was also a small eighteenth century magnifying glass… it was quite small, as large as this (*gesture*)…. And it had two lenses, you see, like all reading-glasses; there were two lenses mounted on a small golden frame, and it was hanging from my chain. Now, between the two glasses I put these petals and I used to carry this about with me always because I wanted to keep it with me; you see, I trusted this lady and knew she had power. I wanted to keep this with me, and I always felt a kind of energy, warmth, confidence, force which came from that thing…. I did not think about it, you see, but I felt it like that.

Divine Love   *A flower which is said to bloom even in the desert.*

And then, one day, suddenly I felt quite depleted, as though a support that was there had gone. Something very unpleasant. I said, "It is strange; what has happened? Nothing really unpleasant has happened to me. Why do I feel like this, so empty, emptied of energy?" And in the evening, when I took off my watch and chain, I noticed that one of the small glasses had come off and all the petals were gone. There was not one petal left. Then I really knew that they carried a considerable charge of power, for I had felt the difference without even knowing the reason. I didn't know the reason and yet it had made a considerable difference. So it was after this that I saw how one could use flowers by charging them with forces. They are extremely receptive.

*

An Old Chaldean Legend

Long, long ago, in the dry land which is now Arabia, a divine being incarnated upon earth to awaken in it the supreme love. As expected it was persecuted by men, misunderstood, suspected, pursued. Mortally wounded by its assailants, it wanted to die quietly in solitude in order to be able to accomplish its work, and being pursued, it ran away. Suddenly, in the vast desert land there appeared a small pomegranate bush. The saviour crept in under the low branches, to leave its body in peace; and immediately the bush spread out miraculously, it grew higher, larger, became deep and thick, so that when the pursuers passed by, they did not even suspect that the One whom they were chasing was hidden there, and they went their way.

While drop by drop the sacred blood fell, fertilising the soil, the bush was covered with marvellous flowers, scarlet, large, crowded with petals…innumerable drops of blood.

These are the flowers which express and contain for us the Divine's Love.

*

Sweet Mother, has that Chaldean legend which you have written any relation with Kali Puja?

Yes, my child, because on Kali Puja day I *always* distribute the flowers of "Divine Love"; for Kali is the most loving of all the aspects of the Mahashakti; here is the most active and most powerful Love. And that is why every year I distribute the petals of "Divine Love" on Kali's Day. And so naturally this explanation of why these flowers were chosen to express the Divine's Love – it is a sufficient explanation.

*

Have flowers a power in the occult world?

Yes, they have an occult power; they can even transmit a message if one knows how to charge them with it.

Can flowers transmit other messages apart from the significances you have given?

It is not impossible but the person who sends the message must have a great power of formation.

Is the power of formation purely occult or can a mental or vital power of formation also transmit messages?

The mental power of formation can certainly transmit messages. But for these messages to be received and understood, the person to whom they are sent must himself be very receptive mentally and particularly attentive.

When we offer flowers, with what attitude should we offer them? Does it matter if we do not know the significance?

This depends completely on the person who gives the flowers and on his state of consciousness. The same answer may be given to both the questions. According to the degree of consciousness of people what they do has a deep significance.

Do flowers retain the force always, even when they decay?

Decay? No, my child; when they dry up, yes. Decayed flowers are just nothing. A decomposition takes place, so the thing disappears. Perhaps it brings energy to the soil, that's quite possible; but still, when it decays it is good only to make manure to grow other flowers. But if it dries up, it is preserved, it can remain for quite a long time.

Sweet Mother, what should we do with the flowers which you give us every day?

Flowers? You ought to keep them as long as they are fresh, and when they are no longer so, you must collect them and give them to the gardener (any gardener you know), so that he can put them in the earth to produce other flowers. Yes, one must give back to the earth what it has given us, for otherwise it will become poor.

THE MOTHER

Each Petal is a Thought

The white Champak flower, Plumeria, is named by the Mother 'Psychological Perfection'. It has five petals. In this beautiful talk the Mother reveals the meaning of each petal and the quality it signifies for the aspiring sadhak and, with a unique psychological insight, throws a new light on the true meaning of each quality. The talk begins with the Mother showing the Champak flower and counting its petals.

Who remembers this?

(*Counting the petals*) One, two, three, four, five psychological perfections. What are the five psychological perfections?

So, if someone knows it, he can tell us, we'll compare….

Aspiration, devotion, sincerity and faith.

That makes only four, so far.

And surrender….

In any case, what is always there, in all combinations and to whomever I give it, the first among them all is sincerity. For if there is no sincerity, one cannot advance even by half a step. So that is the first, and it is always there.

But it is possible to translate it by another word, if you prefer it, which would be "transparency". I shall explain this word:

Someone is in front of me and I am looking at him; I look into his eyes. And if this person is sincere or "transparent", through his eyes I go down and I see his soul – clearly. But – this is precisely the experience – when I look at somebody and see a little cloud, then I continue, I see a screen, and then sometimes it is a wall, and afterwards it is something quite black; and all this must be crossed, and holes bored in order to go through: and even then I am not sure if at the last minute I may not find myself before a door of bronze so thick that I shall never get through and see his soul; so, of such a person I can immediately say that he is not sincere. But I can also say, figuratively, that he is not transparent. That is the first thing.

There is a second, which is obviously as indispensable if you want to go forward; it is to have faith. Or another word, which seems more limited but is for me more important, because (it is a question of experience) if your faith is not made of a complete trust in the Divine, well, you may very easily remain under the impression that you have faith and yet be losing all trust in the divine Power or divine Goodness, or the Trust the Divine has in you. These are the three stumbling-blocks:

Those who have what they call an unshakable faith in the Divine, and say, "It is the Divine who is doing everything, who can do everything; all that happens in me, in others, everywhere, is the work of the Divine and the Divine alone", if they follow this with some kind of logic, after some time they will blame the Divine for all the most terrible wrongs which take place in the world and make of Him a real demon, cruel and frightful – if they have no trust.

Or again, they do have faith, but tell themselves, "Well, I have faith in the Divine, but this world, I see quite well what it's like! First of all, I suffer so much, don't I? I am very unhappy, far more unhappy than all my neighbours" – for one is always far more unhappy than all one's neighbours – "I am very unhappy and, truly, life is cruel to me.

Psychological Perfection

There is not one psychological perfection but five, like the five petals of this flower. We have said they are: sincerity, faith, devotion, aspiration and surrender. But as a matter of fact every time I give this flower it is not always the same psychological perfection. It is something very fluid, depending on the circumstances and the need of people.

Simple Sincerity
The beginning of all progress.

But then the Divine is divine, He is All-Goodness, All-Generosity, All-Harmony, so how is it that I am so unhappy? He must be powerless; otherwise being so good how could He let me suffer so much?"

That is the second stumbling-block.

And the third: there are people who have what may be called a warped and excessive modesty or humility and who tell themselves,

Transparency
Can come only as a result of perfect sincerity.

"Surely the Divine has thrown me out. I a good for nothing, He can do nothing with m the only thing for me is to give up the gam for He finds me unworthy of Him!"

So, unless one adds to faith a total ar complete trust in the Divine Grace, there wi be difficulties. So both are necessary….

Now, we have put "devotion" in this serie Yes, devotion is all very well, but unless it accompanied by many other things it too ma make many mistakes. It may meet with gre difficulties.

Fait
You flame up and triumph

You have devotion, and you keep you ego. And then your ego makes you do all sort of things out of devotion, things which ar terribly egoistic. That is to say, you think onl of yourself, not of others, nor of the world, no of the work, nor of what ought to be done – yo think only of your devotion. And you becom tremendously egoistic. And so, when you fin out that the Divine, for some reason, does no answer to your devotion with the enthusias you expected of Him, you despair and fa back into the same three difficulties I was jus speaking about: either the Divine is cruel – w

Trust in the Divine
Very indispensable for the impulsive vital.

have read that, there are many such stories of enthusiastic devotees who abuse the Divine because He is no longer as gentle and near to them as before, He has withdrawn, " Why hast Thou deserted me? Thou hast abandoned me, O monster!"... They don't dare to say this, but think it, or else they say, "Oh! I must have made such a serious mistake that I am thrown out", and they fall into despair.

Devotion
Modest and fragrant, it gives itself without seeking for anything in return.

But there is another movement which should constantly accompany devotion…. That kind of sense of gratitude that the Divine exists; that feeling of a marvelling thankfulness which truly fills you with a sublime joy at the fact that the Divine exists, that there is something in the universe which is the Divine, that it is not just the monstrosity we see, that there is the Divine, the Divine exists. And each time that the least thing puts you either directly or indirectly in contact with this sublime Reality of divine existence, the heart is filled with so intense, so marvellous a joy, such a gratitude as of all things has the most delightful taste.

Gratitude
It is you who open all the closed doors and let the Grace which saves penetrate deeply.

There is nothing which gives you a joy equal to that of gratitude. One hears a bird sing, sees a lovely flower, looks at a little child, observes an act of generosity, reads a beautiful sentence, looks at the setting sun, no matter what, suddenly this comes upon you, this kind of emotion – indeed so deep, so intense – that the world manifests the Divine, that there is something behind the world which is the Divine.

So I find that devotion without gratitude is quite incomplete, gratitude must come with devotion.

I remember that once we spoke of courage as one of the perfections; I remember having written it down once in a list. But this courage means having a taste for the supreme adventure. And this taste for supreme adventure is aspiration – an aspiration which takes hold of you completely and flings you, without calculation and without reserve and without a possibility of withdrawal, into the great adventure of the divine discovery, the great adventure of the divine meeting, the yet greater adventure of the divine Realisation; you throw yourself into the adventure without looking back and without asking for a single minute, "What's going to happen?" For if you ask what is going to happen, you never start, you always remain stuck there, rooted to the spot, afraid to lose something, to lose your balance.

That's why I speak of courage – but really it is aspiration. They go together. A real aspiration is something full of courage.

And now, surrender. In English the word is "surrender", there is no French word which gives exactly that sense. But Sri Aurobindo has

Aspiration
Innumerable and obstinate, repeating itself untiringly.

said – I think we have read this – that surrender is the first and absolute condition for doing the yoga. So, if we follow what he has said, this is not just one of the necessary qualities: it is the first attitude indispensable for beginning the yoga. If one has not decided to make a total surrender one cannot begin.

But for this surrender to be total, all these qualities are necessary. And I add one more – for so far we have only four – I add endurance. For, if you are not able to face difficulties without getting discouraged and without giving up, because it is too difficult; and if you are incapable…well, of receiving blows and yet continuing, of "pocketing" them, as they say – when you receive blows as a result of your defects, of putting them in your pocket and continuing to go forward without flagging – you don't go very far; at the first turning where you lose sight of your little habitual life, you fall into despair and give up the game.

The most…how shall I put it? the most material form of this is perseverance. Unless you are resolved to begin the same thing over again a thousand times if need be… You know,

Courage
Bold, it faces all dangers.

People have a beautiful experience and say, "Ah, now this is it!..." And then it settles down, diminishes, gets veiled, and suddenly something quite unexpected, absolutely commonplace and apparently completely uninteresting comes before you and blocks your way. And then you say, "Ah! What's the good of having made this progress if it's going to start all over

Endurance
Going to the very end of the effort without fatigue or relaxing.

people come to me in despair, "But I thought it was done and now I must begin again!" And if they are told, "But that's nothing, you will probably have to begin again a hundred times, two hundred times, a thousand times; you take one step forward and think you are secure, but there will always be something to bring back the same difficulty a little farther on. You think you have solved the problem, you must solve it yet once again; it will turn up again looking just a little different, but it will be the same problem", and if you are not determined that: "Even if it comes back a million times, I shall do it a million times, but I shall go through with it", well, you won't be able to do the yoga. This is absolutely indispensable.

Perseverance
The decision to go to the very end.

Faithfulness
We can count on you.
You never fail us when we need you.

again? Why should I do it? I made an effort, I succeeded, achieved something, and now it's as if I had done nothing! It's indeed hopeless." For you have no endurance.

If one has endurance, one says, "It's all right. Good. I shall begin as often as necessary; a thousand times, ten thousand times, a hundred thousand times if necessary, I shall begin again – but I shall go to the end and nothing will have the power to stop me on the way."

This is most necessary. Most necessary.

So here's my proposal; we put surrender first, at the top of the list, that is, we accept what Sri Aurobindo has said – that to do the integral yoga one must first resolve to surrender entirely to the Divine, there is no other way, this is the way. But after that one must have the five psychological virtues, five psychological perfections, and we say that these perfections are:

Sincerity or Transparency
Faith or Trust
(Trust in the Divine, naturally)
Devotion or Gratitude
Courage or Aspiration
Endurance or Perseverance

One form of endurance is faithfulness, faithfulness to one's resolution – being faithful. One has taken a resolution, one is faithful to

Victory
Will triumph over all obstacles.

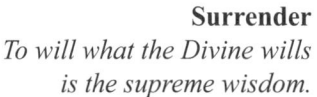

Surrender
*To will what the Divine wills
is the supreme wisdom.*

one's resolution. This is endurance.

There you are.

If one persists, there comes a time when one is victorious.

Victory is to the persistent.

THE MOTHER

*Flower in the crannied wall,
I pluck you out of the crannies,
I hold you here, root and all, in my hand
Little flower – but if I could understand
What you are, root and all, and all in all,
I should know what God and man is.*

Lord Tennyson

The Message of Flowers

The spiritual name of a flower is the message of its soul. Inwardly, the flower is the name itself, "an aspect, an emanation, an aspiration and a progress in the evolution of the earth". Outwardly it is the form and shape, the colour and the number of its petals, its stamens, and the sepals of its calyx. All its various parts have a precise significance. The Mother has pointed out something special about the forms of certain flowers or elaborated on their spiritual significance. These are grouped together in this section.

The Lotus

The red lotus represents Sri Aurobindo, the white represents me.

In a general way the lotus is the flower of the Divine Wisdom – whatever is its colour. But red, it signifies the Avatar – the Divine incarnated in matter, and white, it signifies the Divine Consciousness manifested upon earth.

The Creative Word

Sweet Mother, there's a flower you have named "The Creative Word".
Yes.

The Avatar
The Supreme manifested on earth in a body

What does that mean?

It is the word which creates.

There are all kinds of old traditions, old Hindu traditions, old Chaldean traditions in which the Divine, in the form of the Creator, that is, in His aspect as Creator, pronounces a word which has the power to create. So it is this… And it is the origin of the mantra. The mantra is the spoken word which has a creative power. An invocation is made and there is an answer to the invocation; or one makes a prayer and the prayer is granted. This is the Word, the Word which, in its sound… It is not only the idea, it is in the sound that there's a power of creation. It is the origin, you see, of the mantra.

In Indian mythology the creator God is Brahma, and I think that it was precisely his power which has been symbolised by this flower, "The Creative Word". And when one is in contact with it, the words spoken have a power of evocation or creation or formation or transformation; the words… sound always has a power; it has much more power than men think. It may be a good power and it may be a bad power. It creates vibrations which have an undeniable effect. It is not so much the idea as the sound; the idea too has its own power, but in its own domain – whereas the sound has a power in the material world.

Transformation
The goal of creation.

Transformation

Do you know the flower I have called "Transformation"? Yes. You know it has four petals; well, these four petals are arranged like a cross: one at the top which represents the transcendent, two on each side: the universal, and one at the bottom: the individual.

The petal at the top is divided into two.

Exactly, the transcendent is one and two (or dual) at the same time. This flower is almost perfect in its form. This was the original meaning of the cross also, but that was not as perfect as the flower, for it was one, two, and three. It was not so good – the flower is perfect.

Supramental Psychological Perfection

Have you noticed this flower?

It has twelve petals in three rows of four. We have called it "Supramental Psychological Perfection".

I had never noticed that it has three rows: a small row like this, another one a little larger and a third one larger still. They are in gradation of four: four petals, four petals, four petals.

Well, if one indeed wants to see in the forms of Nature a symbolic expression, one can see a centre which is the supreme Truth, and a triple manifestation – because four indicates manifestation – in three superimposed worlds: the outermost – these are the largest petals, the lightest in colour – that is a physical world, then a vital world and a mental world, and then at the centre, the supramental Truth.

Supramentalised Psychological Perfection
A psychological perfection aspiring to be divinised.

Concentration

Here is a bunch of *Concentration* and of *New Birth*.

To concentrate for developing the intelligence, for developing the inborn faculties which are hidden within ourselves.

To concentrate means to find oneself. It is the quest, the means to follow. It is the shortest way to get anything. One only has to concentrate – but deep within – and toc! You get the thing, the word, the idea, the feeling, the place you want to discover, the plane of consciousness, and with perseverance and a constant effort, find the Self and the soul. To concentrate in order to find the soul. With the help of concentration, one can achieve everything.

But one has to know how to concentrate, and each plane has a certain level of concentration. To know how to concentrate is to acquire the power to withdraw from all other things except the one thing you wish to achieve.

Do you know what you should do? To start with: you sit before a wall and say to yourself: "Let my mind be as white as the wall." Then, if you see a little black dot on the wall, – or anywhere else, – a dot, you start concentrating on this dot, with an intent gaze, without allowing any other thoughts to come into your mind, without moving, without wavering as if you wanted to envelop this dot with your hypnotic gaze. Then you will see that you begin to have a relation with this dot and that nothing else around exists any longer. Only the dot exists, and yourself, attracted as if by a magnet. You have a penetrating gaze. Then, little by little, the black dot doesn't exist in your gaze any more; you are concentrating very hard. But instead of a black dot, there is a luminous dot; as if everything were appearing differently. The black dot has become a luminous dot. And one can see other movements just around this luminous dot. Then, only the luminous dot is seen and nothing else around. And a kind of deep relation is being established. You are going to try and tell me.

Then, if one learns how to concentrate even more, really concentrate with intensity, one perceives that it is not oneself who is concentrating, and that the ego does not exist any longer, but that an altogether detached will, – without thoughts, unflickering, a sort of emptiness but well sustained by the aspiration, – is acting through the so-called self. For the Self seems to be hidden. But the concentration is well directed, deeply fixed there, within (*Mother shows the psychic centre*), undisturbed by the outward happenings, discovering regions of happiness where the divine sweetness reigns. One discovers layer after layer of planes of consciousness, and one leaves behind oneself the subtle bodies, one after another, until there is no more resistance and the soul reveals itself before us, without any agent, without any foreign support. And one discovers the soul in its plenitude. If one starts living in such a way, then one lives forever a new birth. At each moment, one discovers a new life, a new aspiration, a new light and a new love. One springs forward, to always discover something new. That is life.

Concentration
*Does not aim for any effect,
but is simple and persistent.*

One has to know how to concentrate by going deeply there within, to find the inner seat from where one should aspire more and more and, at the same time, reject all that disturbs – the impulses, the sensations, and the thoughts. All that does not belong to us has to be rejected, so that we may be pure in order to identify ourselves with the Divine Consciousness. Three stages that help one another: to concentrate, to reject, and to aspire for the identification with the Divine.

Then you concentrate in the heart, and you aspire to come into contact with the flame, the psychic flame, the flame of purification and go there, very deeply, and remain silent and open like this (*Mother opens Her hands like a flower above Her head*). Once there – but you must sincerely make a great effort to find it, – you are in contact with the central being; everything else becomes silent, and one has the feeling that the Divine is doing everything for oneself. An immutable joy and peace and freedom then seize you. And nothing in the world is interesting any more, but the aspiration that unites with the Divine.

Aspiration in the Physical for the Divine Love

Here is the flower we have called "Aspiration in the Physical for the Divine Love." By the "Physical" I mean the physical consciousness, the most ordinary outward-going consciousness, the normal consciousness of most human beings, which sets such great store by comfort, good food, good clothes, happy relationships, etc., instead of aspiring for the higher things. Aspiration in the physical for the Divine's Love implies that the physical asks for nothing else save that it should feel how the Divine loves it. It realises that all its usual satisfactions are utterly insufficient. But there cannot be a compromise: if the physical wants the Divine's Love it must want that alone and not say, "I shall have the Divine's Love and at the same time keep my other attachments, needs and enjoyments...."

The fundamental seat of aspiration from which it radiates or manifests in one part of the being or another is the psychic centre. When I speak of aspiration in the physical I mean that the very consciousness in you which hankers after material comfort and well-being should of itself, without being compelled by the higher parts of your nature, ask exclusively for the

Aspiration
*Innumerable and obstinate,
repeating itself untiringly.*

Aspiration

Well, today is something special. And these two flowers are just fine: Concentration in the Aspiration... But do you know how to aspire? Do you aspire a little?

Do you know where the aspiration comes from?

Yes, Mother, from the heart and from the psychic.

Yes, my little one, rather from the psychic, the true aspiration comes from there; but one first starts from the heart.

As long as you are not in contact with it, in the beginning you can aspire from the mind saying: Ma, Ma, Ma, Ma, and asking precisely what you want, as, for example, Peace, or let Peace be established within me. Then you silently concentrate and you remain open. You will see that you will be flooded with Peace.

Divine's Love. Usually you have to show it the Light by means of your parts; surely this has to be done persistently, otherwise the physical would never learn and it would take Nature's common round of ages before it learns by itself. Indeed the round of Nature is intended to show it all possible sorts of satisfactions and by exhausting them convince it that none of them can really satisfy it and that what it is at bottom seeking is a divine satisfaction. In Yoga we hasten this slow process of Nature and insist on the physical consciousness seeing the truth and learning to recognise and want it. But how to show it the truth? Well, just as you bring a light into a dark room. Illumine the darkness of your physical consciousness with the intuition and aspiration of your more refined parts and keep on doing so till it realises how futile and unsatisfactory is its hunger for the low ordinary things, and turns spontaneously towards the truth. When it does turn, your whole life will be changed – the experience is unmistakable.

When, as a child, I used to complain to my mother about food or any such small matter she would always tell me to go and do my work or pursue my studies instead of bothering about trifles. She would ask me if I had the complacent idea that I was born for comfort. "You are born to realise the highest Ideal," she would say and send me packing. She was quite right, though of course her notion of the highest Ideal was rather poor by our standards. We are all born for the highest Ideal: therefore, whenever in our Ashram some petty request for more comfort and material happiness is refused, it is for your own good and to make you fulfil what you are here for. The refusal is actually a favour inasmuch as you are thereby considered worthy to stand before the highest ideal and be shaped according to it.

Aspiration in the Physical for the Divine Love
Manifold and intense, difficult to satisfy.

Mental Simplicity *Does not like complications.*

Simplicity

As soon as all effort disappears from a manifestation, it becomes very simple, with the simplicity of a flower opening, manifesting its beauty and spreading its fragrance without clamour or vehement gesture. And in this simplicity lies the greatest power, the power which is least mixed and least gives rise to harmful reactions. The power of the vital should be mistrusted, it is a tempter on the path of the work, and there is always a risk of falling into its trap, for it gives you the taste of immediate results; and, in our first eagerness to do the work well, we let ourselves be carried away to make use of this power. But very soon it deflects all our action from the right course and introduces a seed of illusion and death into what we do.

Simplicity, simplicity! How sweet is the purity of Thy presence!

Eternal Youth and Eternal Smile

There, there, I have kept something for you carefully; as soon as I received these flowers this morning, I thought of you: "It will be something for Mona when he comes." I kept them separately. Do you know what they mean?

This one is *Eternal Youth*, and that one, *Eternal Smile*.

These are two flowers that complete one another. Two flowers that are very essential for a complete life.

If one remains young eternally and if one can smile eternally, then one takes a great step towards transformation. When one is above the fetters of the ego and the desires, one starts smiling, and when one can keep a constant aspiration for progress, then one remains young. Here are two sure means to reach the

Eternal Youth
*It is a gift the Divine gives us
when we unite ourselves with Him.*

goal. Don't waste time. Become an optimist and follow the direct path. There is no need to think.

Successful Future

Do you know what the flower which we have called "Successful Future" signifies when given to you? It signifies the hope – nay, even the promise – that you will participate in the descent of the supramental world. For that descent will be the successful consummation of our work, a descent of which the full glory has not yet been or else the whole face of life would have been different. By slow degrees the Supramental is exerting its influence, now one part of the being and now another feels the embrace or the touch of its divinity; but when it comes down in all its self-existent power, a supreme radical change will seize the whole nature. We are moving nearer and nearer the hour of its complete triumph. Once the world-conditions are ready the full descent will take place carrying everything before it. Its presence will be unmistakable, its force will brook no resistance, doubts and difficulties will not torture you any longer. For the Divine will stand manifest – unveiled in its total perfection. I do not, however, mean to say that the whole world will at once feel its presence or be transformed, but I do mean that a part of humanity will know and participate in its descent – say, this little world of ours here. From there the transfiguring grace will most effectively radiate. And, fortunately for the aspirants, that successful future will materialise for them in spite of all the obstacles set in its way by unregenerate human nature!

THE MOTHER

Successful future
Full of promise and joyous surprises.

The Meaning of Colours

Flowers and colours. Colours and flowers. They always go together. The scientists have given many biological and botanical reasons to explain the colours, but there is also a spiritual reason. In yogic psychology every plane of consciousness has its own particular colour. Flowers with certain colours have often spiritual meanings corresponding to that plane of consciousness.
	Let us take the major planes and their corresponding colours:
* *Physical – bright red*
* *Vital – Dark red – lavender – violet or purple*
* *Mental – Yellow or greenish yellow*
* *Psychic – Pink or pale rose*
* *Supramental – Orange or golden yellow*
* *Integral – White*
* *Krishna's or Sri Aurobindo's Light – Light blue.*
	Here are some flowers which show strikingly the truth of this yogic perception. Many red flowers, for example, are connected with an aspiration in the physical. We must, however, always bear in mind that there is no fixed rule, for truth is beyond all mental laws and formulations.

Aspiration in the Physical
Manifold, simple and joyful.

"What is it in a flower which makes it take and reflect a certain colour?

The scientists say that it is the composition of its atoms but I say that it is the nature of its aspiration.

THE MOTHER

Flowers where the spiritual significance is closely related to the colour

Physical

No. Spiritual Name – (Botanical Name)

1. Aspiration in the physical (Ixora coccinea 'Bandhuca')
2. Aspiration in the physical for the Divine Love (Russelia equisetiformis)
3. Connection between the Light and the physical centre (Canna)
4. Conversion of the physical (Hippeastrum)
5. Dignity in the physical (Dahlia)
6. Generosity in the physical (Impatiens balsamina)
7. Joyous physical enthusiasm (Petunia hybrida)
8. Offering of the physical (Althaea rosea)
9. Opening of the physical to the Divine Love (Quamoclit coccinea)
10. Physical aspiration for immortality (Celosia argentea)
11. Physical boldness (Celosia argentea 'Cristata')
12. Physical centre (Canna)
13. Physical consciousness entirely turned towards the Divine (Tithonia rotundifolia)
14. Physical continuity (Acalypha hispida)
15. Physical curiosity (Holmskioldia sanguinea)
16. Physical endurance (Zinnia)
17. Physical enthusiasm (Petunia hybrida)
18. Physical protection (Bougainvillea)
19. Physical receptivity (Gladiolus)
20. Physical thoroughness (Verbena hybrida)
21. Power of physical expression (Antirrhinum majus)
22. Skill in physical work (Phlox drummondii)
23. Spiritual aspiration in the physical (Russelia coccinea)
24. Transparency in the physical (Callistephus chinensis)

Vital

No. Spiritual Name – (Botanical Name)

1. Aspiration for vital purity (Duranta erecta)
2. Broadening of the most material vital (Sinningia speciosa)
3. Conscious vital immortality (Gomphrena Globosa)
4. Correct movement in the vital (Saintpaulia ionantha)
5. Distinction of the vital (Melia azedarach)
6. Endurance of the higher vital (Zinnia)
7. Enthusiasm in the most material vital (Petunia hynrida)
8. Enthusiasm in the higher vital (Petunia hybrida)
9. Formative faculty in the vital (Crotalaria spectabilis)
10. Intimacy with the Divine in the vital (Lagerstroemia indica)
11. Joyous enthusiasm in the most material vital (Petunia hybrida)
12. Krishna's light in the vital (Ruellia tuberosa)
13. Life energy in the vital (Chrysanthemum morifolium)
14. Light in the vital (Cestrum purpureum)
15. Opening of the material vital to the light (Thunbergia erecta)
16. Power of vital expression (Antirrhinum majus)
17. Radha's consciousness in the vital (Clitoria ternatea)
18. Renunciation of vital desires (Angelonia grandiflora)
19. Seeking the light in the lower vital (Iochroma cyaneum)
20. Silence in the vital (Achimenes grandiflora)
21. Skill in vital work (Phlox drummondii)
22. Supramentalised vital transparency (Callistephus chinensis)
23. Transparency of the emotive vital (Callistephus chinensis)
24. Vital aspiration for immortality (Celosia argentea)
25. Vital attachment for the divine (Spathoglottis plicata)
26. Vital consecration (Heliotropium peruvianum)
27. The vital governed by the presence (Setcreasea purpurea)
28. Vital courage (Solanum trilobatum)
29. Vital endurance (Zinnia)
30. Vital enthusiasm (Petunia hybrida)
31. Vital immortality (Gomphrena globosa)
32. Vital joy in matter (Nierembergia caerulea)
33. Vital protection (Bougainvillea)
34. Vital receptivity (Gladiolus)
35. Vital thoroughness (verbena hybrida)
36. Vital transparency (Callistephus chinensis)

Vital sensitivity
Is excessive if not controlled.

Mental

No. Spiritual Name – (Botanical Name)

1. Birth of true mental sincerity (Melampodium)
2. First mental awakening in matter (Tribulus terrestris)
3. Mental aspiration (Ixora lutea)
4. Mental attachment for the Divine (Dendrobium moschatum)
5. Mental balance (Begonia)
6. Mental boldness (Celosia argentea 'Cristata')
7. Mental cheerfulness (Gaillardia pulchella 'Picta')
8. Mental curiosity (Holmskioldia sanguinea)
9. Mental endurance (Zinnia)
10. Mental goodwill (Mussaenda luteola)
11. Mental gratitude (Ipomoea tuberose)
12. Mental honesty (Tristellateia australis)
13. Mental love for the Divine (Rosa)
14. Mental love under the psychic influence (Rosa)
15. Mental opening (Barleria prionitis)
16. Mental plasticity (Tagetes erecta)
17. Mental prayer (Zephyranthes sulphurea)
18. Mental promise (Abutilon)
19. Mental receptivity (Gladiolus)
20. Mental simplicity (Thymophylla tenuiloba)
21. Mental sincerity (Solidago)
22. Mental spirit of imitation (Loranthus)
23. Mental suggestions of organization (Aglaia odorata)
24. Mental tapasya (Datura)
25. Mental trust in the Divine (Asystasia coromandeliana)
26. Mental voice (Gmelina)
27. Perfect mental balance (Begonia)
28. Power of mental expression (Antirrhinum majus)

Mental Sincerity
The essential condition for integral honesty.

Psychic

No. Spiritual Name – (Botanical Name)

1. First emergence of the psychic in matter (Jatropha multifida)
2. Intimacy with the Divine in the psychic (Lagerstroemia indica)
3. Joyous psychic enthusiasm (Petunia hybrida)
4. Perfect psychic balance (Begonia)
5. Power of psychic expression (Antirrhinum majus)
6. Power of the psychic consciousness (Hibiscus)
7. Psychic aspiration (Ixora chinensis 'Rosea')
8. Psychic balance (Begonia)
9. Psychic centre (Canna)
10. Psychic endurance (Zinnia)
11. Psychic enthusiasm (Petunia hybrida)
12. Psychic generosity (Impatiens balsamina)
13. Psychic influence in the emotions (Beloperone oblongata)
14. Psychic light in the physical movements (Pentas lanceolata)
15. Psychic light in the subconscient (Crossandra)
16. Psychic offering (Althaea rosea)
17. Psychic power in existence (Hibiscus)
18. Psychic prayer (Habranthus robustus)
19. Psychic protection (Bougainvillea)
20. Psychic receptivity (Gladiolus)
21. Psychic soaring of nature (Rosa canina)
22. Psychic thoroughness (Verbena hybrida)
23. Psychic transparency (Callistephus chinensis)
24. Psychic work (Cassia javanica)
25. Psycho-physical generosity (Impatiens balsamina)
26. Skill in psychic work (Phlox drummondii)

Psychic Balance
Under the psychic influence all activity becomes balanced.

Supramental Immortality upon earth
This remains to be realised.

Supramental

No. Spiritual Name – (Botanical Name)

1. The body-consciousness undergoing the supramental transformation (Helianthus)
2. Consciousness turned towards the supramental light (Helianthus)
3. Future supramental centre (Canna)
4. Matter prepares itself to receive the supramental (Erythrina indica 'Parcellii')
5. Matter under the supramental guidance (Hamelia patens)
6. Power of the supramental consciousness (Hibiscus)
7. Success in supramental work (Cochlospermum religiosa)
8. Supramental attachment for the Divine (Rosa 'Father's day')
9. Supramental beauty in the physical (Hibiscus)
10. Supramental bird (Strelitzia regina)
11. Supramental immortality (Gomphrena globosa)
12. Supramental influence (Doxantha unguis-cati)
13. Supramental influence in the subconscient (Crossandra)
14. Supramental rain (Pyrostegia venusta)
15. Supramental sun (Anthocephalus indicus)
16. Supramentalised endurance (Zinnia)
17. Supramentalised life energy (Chrysanthemum morifolium)
18. Supramentalised mental dignity (Dahlia)
19. Supramentalised plasticity (Tagetes erecta)
20. Supramentalised psychological perfection (Michelia champaca)
21. Supramentalised receptivity (Gladiolus)

Integral

No. Spiritual Name – (Botanical Name)

1. Aspiration for integral immortality (Aerva javanica)
2. Balanced use of the integral power (Sinningia speciosa)
3. Integral attachment for the Divine (Spathoglottis plicata)
4. Integral conversion (Hippeastrum)
5. Integral courage (Calotropis procera 'Alba')
6. Integral endurance (Zinnia)
7. Integral enthusiasm (Petunia hybrida)
8. Integral even basis in the physical (Clerodendrum fragrans)
9. Integral gratitude (Operculina turpethum)
10. Integral harmony (Antigonon leptopus 'Album')
11. Integral Immortality (Gomphrena globosa)
12. Integral intimacy with the Divine (Lagerstroemia indica)
13. Integral mental purity (Tabernaemontana coronaria)
14. Integral offering (Althaea rosea)
15. Integral offering of the vital (Althaea rosea)
16. Integral opening of the being towards the Divine (Barleria cristata)
17. Integral opening to the light (Thunbergia erecta)
18. Integral organisation (Pseuderanthemum)
19. Integral prayer (Zephyranthes candida)
20. Integral progress (Catharanthus roseus)
21. Integral psychological perfection (Plumeria obtusa)
22. Integral purity (Jasminum)
23. Integral receptivity (Gladiolus)
24. Integral renunciation of the vital desires (Angelonia grandiflora)
25. Integral revelation (Costus Sp.)
26. Integral silence (Passiflora foetida)
27. Integral simplicity (Vittadinia)
28. Integral solace (Mirabilis jalapa)
29. Integral tapasya (Datura)
30. Integral thoroughness (Verbena hybrida)
31. Integral transparency (Callistephus chinensis)
32. Integral trust in the Divine (Asystasia coromandeliana)
33. Integral wealth of Mahalakshmi (Nymphaea)
34. Integral wisdom (Albizia lebbeck)
35. Joy of integral faithfulness (Portlandia grandiflora)
36. Joy of integral peace (Crinum)
37. Joyous integral enthusiasm (Petunia hybrida)
38. Peace of integral faithfulness (Portlandia grandiflora)
39. Power of integral purity (Hibiscus)
40. Skill of integral work (Phlox drummondii)
41. Striving towards integral wisdom (Calliandra hematocephala)
42. Unconditional integral offering (Ipomoea tricolor 'pearly gates')

Integral Offering
The surest road to realisation.

Fragrant Flowers

Quiet and alone in a garden! A sweet fragrance fills your being. You are drawn to it and, like a child's gentle hands, it guides you to its source. And you find yourself standing before a creeper of pure white jasmines.

Or you are drawn to a column of gold, streaming with flowers. It is the Indian Laburnum, in full bloom of its 'Imagination' flowers. Perhaps, a golden light was descending upon earth and these trees by their aspiration have drawn it, like a magnet, to themselves. And they are completely illumined. Now they scatter their splendour of light and the fragrance all around.

Colour, form and fragrance are the three inherent attributes of a flower. Of these, fragrance is the generous self-giving of flowers.

Do the strong-scented flowers represent a more ardent psychic prayer than the unscented ones?

Their nature gives itself more generously and more integrally.

*

Is there a relation between the perfume of a flower and its significance?

Certainly there should be one. But so far I have not studied it.

*

How can one begin to study this relation? What is the first step?

Study and experience. You take a flower with a strong and definite perfume. You breathe in this perfume, trying to find what thought or image it evokes. If you find something, you compare it with the significance given to the flower. It is a long and detailed work. After some hundreds of experiences one may arrive at a conclusion.

When animality will drop off, then absolute necessity of food also will drop off. And there will probably be a transition when one will have less and less purely material food.

For example, when you smell flowers it is nourishing. I have seen it, you nourish yourself in a more subtle way.

THE MOTHER

Correct self-evaluation
*Simple and modest,
does not try to push itself forward.*

Some fragrant flowers

No.	Spiritual Name	Common name (India)	Common name (West)	Botanical name
1.	Air	Raat ki rani	Night queen	Cestrum nocturnum
2.	Alchemy		Spider Lily	Hymenocallis
3.	Aspiration	Parijata	Night Jasmine	Nyctanthes arbor-tristis
4.	Clear mind		Climbing Ylang-ylang	Artabotrys odoratissimus
5.	Correct self-evaluation		Yellow jasmine	Jasminum prumila
6.	Divine smile	Champaka	Yellow champa	Michelia champaca 'Alba'
7.	Energy turned towards the Divine	Mehndi	Hennah	Lawsonia inermis
8.	Entire self-giving		Moon flower	Calonyction aculeatum
9.	Faithfulness	Madhumalati	Rangoon creeper	Quisqualis indica
10.	Humility before the Divine in the physical nature			Pavetta thomsonii
11.	Integral purity	Mogra	Jasmine	Jasminum
12.	Joy of integral faithfulness		White horse flower	Portlandia grandiflora
13.	Miracle	Alli	Ironwood tree	Memecylon edule
14.	Modesty		Sweet violet	Viola odorata
15.	New birth		Sweet marjoram	Oreganum majorana
16.	Patience	Bokul	Spanish cherry	Mimusops elengi
17.	Peace in the cells			Ixora parviflora
18.	Peace in the physical	Sultana champa	Alexandrian laurel	Calophyllum inophyllum
19.	Peace in the vital	Kamini	Orange jasmine	Murraya paniculata
20.	Prosperity	Nagalingam	Canonball tree	Couroupita guianensis
21.	Psychological perfection	Chameli	Temple tree	Plumeria
22.	Radiating purity	Gandharaj	Cape jasmine	Gardenia jasminoides
23.	Satchidananda	Dulaba champa	Ginger lily	Hedychium
24.	Service	Iyavakai	Copper pod	Peltaphorum pterocarpum
25.	Silence	Kaurav Pandav	Blue crown passion flower	Passiflora caerulea
26.	Spiritual atmosphere	Neem	Margosa	Azadirachta indica
27.	Spiritual perfume	Kewada	Screw pine	Pandanus tectorius
28.	Spiritual success	Madhavilata		Hiptage benghalensis
29.	Straightforwardness	Rukmini	Torch tree	Ixora arborea
30.	Supramentalised psychological perfection	Champak	Golden champa	Michelia champaca
31.	Surrender	Gulab	Country rose	Rosa
32.	Sweetness of thought exclusively turned towards the Divine	Kaner	Oleander	Nerium Odorum
33.	The New Creation		Tuberose	Polianthes tuberosa
34.	Transformation	Akash neem	Indian cork tree	Millingtonia hortensis
35.	Wealth		Water lily	Nymphaea

Joy of Integral Faithfulness
*That link of love which makes
all faithfulness so easy.*

Satchidananda
*Strong and pure, it stands erect
with its creative power.*

Silence
The ideal condition for progress.

Purity
True purity gives a lovely fragrance.

Flowers leave some of their fragrance in the hand that bestows them.
Chinese Proverb

45

A Child's Aspiration

What should a child aspire for? Here is its aspiration in the language of flowers.

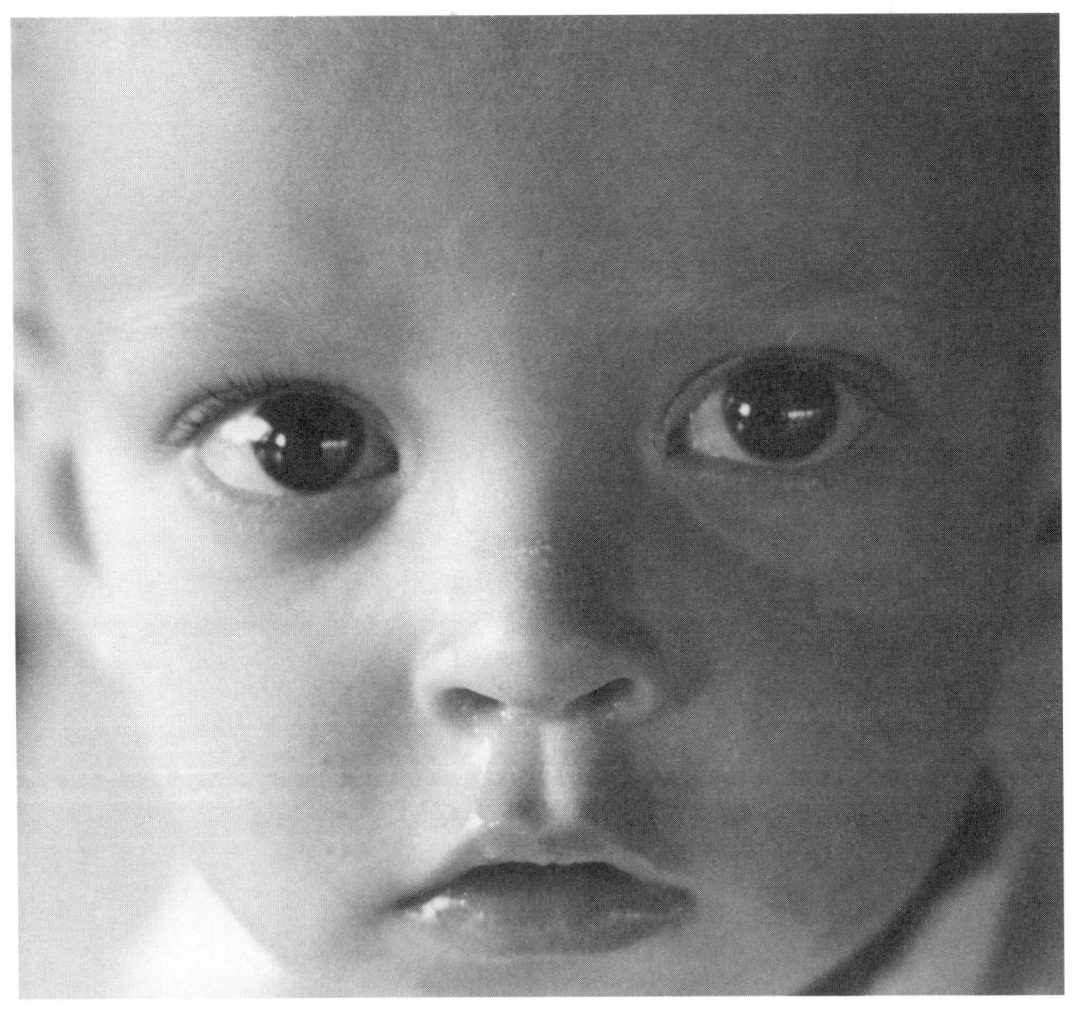

If thou wouldst attain to thy highest, go look upon a flower; what that does will-lessly, that do thou willingly.
                              Friedrich von Schiller

Eternal Youth
It is a gift the Divine gives us when we unite ourselves with Him.

A child's aspiration expressed through flowers.

What I aspire to have in my Heart

No.	Spiritual Name	Common name (India)	Common name (West)	Botanical name
1.	Faith			Hibiscus albo-variegate
2.	Simple sincerity		Aster	Aster amellus
3.	Integral simplicity		Creeping Daisy	Vittadinia
4.	Humility		Drop seed	Sporobolus capillaris
5.	Gratitude			Ipomoea carnea
6.	Thirst for perfection		Shrimp plant	Beloperone guttata
7.	Trust in the Divine			Asystasia coromandeliana
8.	Eternal youth			Hibiscus miniatus
9.	Integral immortality		Globe amarant	Gomphrena globosa
10.	Certitude of victory		Lily thorn	Catesbaea spinosa
11.	Successful future		Blanket flower	Gaillardia pulchella 'Lorenziana'
12.	Friendship with the Divine		Indian Shot	Canna indica
13.	Constant remembrance of the Divine		Japanese Honeysuckle	Lonicera japonica

Cheerfulness
A joyous smile of Nature.

What I aspire to have in my Nature

No.	Spiritual Name	Common name (India)	Common name (West)	Botanical name
1.	Cheerfulness			Gaillardia pulchella 'Picta'
2.	Happy heart		Lemonia	Ravenia spectabilis
3.	Enthusiasm		Petunia	Petunia hybrida
4.	Generosity		Balsam	Impatiens balsamina
5.	Frankness		Transvael Daisy	Gerbera jamesonii
6.	Straightforwardness	Rukmini	Torch tree	Ixora arborea
7.	Unselfishness		Harold's trumpet	Beaumontia jerdoniana
8.	Mental honesty			Tristellateia australisiae
9.	Absolute truthfulness		Chalice wine	Solandra hartwegii
10.	Refinement of habits	Konamaram	Madre	Gliricidia sepium
11.	Dignity			Dahlia
12.	Nobility			Dahlia
13.	Aspiration for the right attitude		Glory bower	Clerodendrum speciosum
14.	Harmony		Coral creeper	Antigonon leptopus
15.	Modesty		Sweet Violet	Viola odorata
16.	Eternal smile			Hibiscus miniatus
17.	Transparency		China Aster	Callistephus chinensis
18.	Gentleness		Sweet Pea	Lathyrus odoratus

Determination
Knows what it wants and does it.

What I aspire to have in my Body and Vital

No. Spiritual Name	Common name (India)	Common name (West)	Botanical name
1. Health	Bhendi	Portia tree	Thespesia populnea
2. Patience	Bokul	Spanish cherry	Mimusops elengi
3. Endurance		Zinnia	Zinnia
4. Perseverance		Pot marigold	Calendula officinalis
5. Control			Billbergia sp.
6. Will one with the Divine Will		Rose of Sharon	Hibiscus syriacus
7. Determination			Kopsia fruiticosa
8. Bravery		Amaranth	Amaranthus bicolor
9. Boldness		Cockscomb	Celosia argentia 'Cristata'
10. Steadfastness	Amrud	Guava	Psidium guajava
11. Fearlessness			Solanum torvum
12. Courage	Mudar		Calotropis procera
13. Refined taste			Kaempferia galanga

Imagination
Abundant and varied, may be charming, but must not be substituted for the Truth.

What I aspire to have in my Mind

No.	Spiritual Name	Common name (India)	Common name (West)	Botanical name
1.	Concentration		Crown of thorns	Euphorbia millii
2.	Imagination	Amaltas	Golden shower tree	Cassia fistula
3.	Resolution		Lady of the night	Brunfelsia americana
4.	Organisation			Pseuderanthemum
5.	Curiosity		Cup-and- saucer plant	Holmskioldia sanguinea
6.	Never tell a lie			Pereskia
7.	Power of expression		Snap dragon	Antirrhinum majus
8.	Clear mind		Climbing Ylang-Ylang	Artabotrys odoratissimus
9.	Quiet mind	Kanel	Sweet-scented oleander	Nerium oleander
10.	Common sense		Tobacco Flower	Nicotiana alata 'Grandiflora'
11.	Eloquence		Shell Flower	Alpinia speciosa
12.	To know how to listen			Podranea picasoliana
13.	To know what is to be said		Cardamom	Alpinia speciosa
14.	The thirst to learn		Spanish Flag	Quamoclit lobata
15.	Thirst to understand		Chinese Lavender	Crossostephium artemesioides
16.	Integrally pure thoughts		Pansy	Viola tricolor hortensis
17.	Accurate perception		Ylang-Ylang	Cananga odorata
18.	Logic in thoughts		Mesquite	Prosopis glandulosa torreyiana

Service

To be at the Divine's service is the surest means of attaining realisation.

What I aspire to have in my Work

No.	Spiritual Name	Common name (India)	Common name (West)	Botanical name
1.	Thoroughness		Perennial verbena	Verbena hybrida
2.	Regularity		Tiger-claw plant	Martynia annua
3.	Discipline		Basil	Ocimum basilicum
4.	Care		Spider plant	Chlorophytum clatum vittatum
5.	Obedience		Chinese pink	Dianthus chinensis
6.	Collaboration		Carnation	Dianthus caryophyllus
7.	Progress	Sadabahar		Vinca roseus
8.	Service	Iyavakai	Copper pod	Peltaphorum pterocarpum
9.	Fearlessness in action		Love-lies-bleeding	Amaranthus caudatus
10.	Skill in works			Phlox drummondii
11.	Cheerful endeavour		African daisy	Arctotis stoechadifolia 'Grandis'
12.	Faultless planning of work			Clerodendrum inerme
13.	Artistic work			Phlox drummondii
14.	Works of love		Perennial Balsam	Impatiens walleriana
15.	Heroic action			Ruellia makoyana
16.	Enthusiasm in action			Petunia hybrida

The Roses!

No book on flowers can ever be complete without them – the Roses. Poets through the ages have not ceased to sing of their beauty, their splendour, their magnificence. They have been expressions of human love in every language and country and, much more deeply, they express 'Love for the Divine'. This is also their spiritual meaning, though the emphasis may change with variations in size, colour, shape and fragrance.

Some roses and their spiritual meanings.

Spiritual Name	Description
1. Love for the Divine	All roses in general
2. Human passions changed into love for the Divine	Red roses
3. Mental love for the Divine	Yellow roses
4. Mental love under the psychic influence	Cream or yellow roses tinged pink
5. Flaming love for the Divine	Orange roses
6. Humility in the love for the Divine	Lavender or mauve roses
7. Balance of the nature in the love for the Divine	Bicoloured roses
8. Integral love for the Divine	Solitary pure white roses
9. Surrender	Country rose, highly fragrant pink roses
10. Mental surrender	Yellow roses tinged orange
11. Pure spiritual surrender	Small white roses in full pendulous clusters
12. Loving surrender	Fully double medium to large solitary pink roses except 'Surrender' and 'Perfect Surrender'
13. Detailed surrender	Fairy Queen roses, tiny pink roses
14. Perfect surrender	Highly fragrant large double pink roses
15. Supramental attachment for the Divine	Small light orange roses in small clusters
16. Timidity in attachment for the Divine	Small green roses
17. Communion with the Divine	Dense erect clusters of single or double roses, all colours
18. Affection for the Divine	White roses tinged pink
19. Psychic soaring of nature	Dog rose, Eglantine, clusters of fragrant light pink single roses
20. Beauty offering itself in the service of the Divine	Salmon-coloured roses

**The One, in his glory multitudinous,
Bursting into shape and colour like a rose,
Compels the great world-petals to unclose.**

SRI AUROBINDO

The Elements

Amongst the flowers named by the Mother there are some which correspond to the elements – Water, Air, Fire, Ether. There are also a few like Light, Flame, Agni or Silver and Gold.

Flowers as Elements

No.	Spiritual Name	Common name (India)	Common name (West)	Botanical name
1.	Water		Bridal Creeper	Porana paniculata
2.	Air	Raat-ki-Rani	Night queen	Cestrum nocturnum
3.	Light	Din-ka-Raja	Queen of the Day	Cestrum diurnum
4.	Ether		Horse-tail creeper	Porana volubilis
5.	Fire	Krishnachura	Peacock flower	Poinciana pulcherrima
6.	Flame		Coral hibiscus	Hibiscus schizopetalus
7.	Agni			Hibiscus
8.	Gold	Kanchan	St. Thomas tree	Bauhinia tomentosa
9.	Silver		Brisbane lily	Eurycles sylvestris

Fire   *Fears no obstacle.*

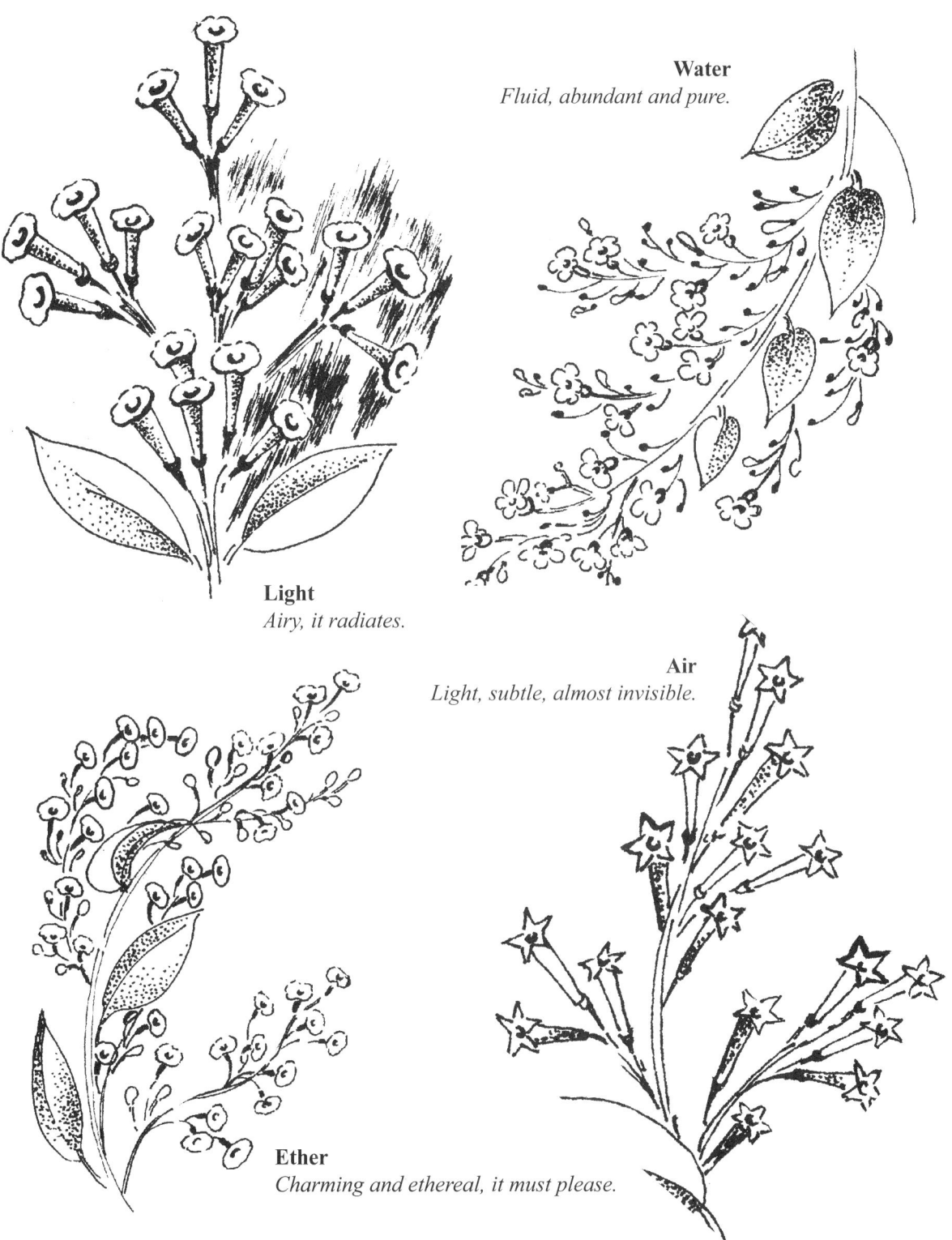

Some striking Patterns

When we look at the spiritual significance given to flowers by the Mother, we are struck by certain rhythms, certain patterns and structures. Interesting combinations and relations appear. Some of them may be merely the superimposition of our mind but some may also have a deeper significance. These patterns do not always hold but still they provide some interesting insights:

There are some flowers which have both, single and multiple petals. The multiple petalled flowers are often qualified as "Perfect".

There are others, large and small, which come in two distinct sizes. The smaller flower is frequently called "Detailed".

When the flowers are in several separate colours, then the multi-coloured variety is described as "Manifold".

There are some flowers which grow in the wild and which we hardly notice. Or even if we see them we tend to overlook them. They have some very beautiful meanings. Among the 'wild' flowers we have 'Gratitude', 'Humility', 'Straightforwardness', 'Lightness' and the 'Touch me not', which is 'Vital Sensitivity'.

The dahlias are found in different sizes, shapes and colours, single and multipetalled. It is fascinating to observe how the meaning too changes and evolves. The smallest dahlias with a hard big centre and small single petals are 'Vanity'. The small double or multiple petalled dahlias are called 'Pride'. The medium size dahlias are named 'Dignity' and the large dark red ones are 'Nobility'. The very large flowers in several colours, often with curved petals, signify 'Aristocracy' and finally the very large, pure white dahlias are called 'Superhumanity'. An amazing evolution: Vanity, Pride, Dignity, Nobility, Aristocracy, Superhumanity.

There are some flowers connected with the faculty of speech which make an interesting study when grouped together. They are:

* 'To know what is to be said' [Alpinia galanza]
* 'To know how to listen' [Podranea ricasotiana]
* 'Never tell a lie' [Peraskia]

And here are some flowers whose very names would appeal to poets and artists. In fact one flower is even called 'Poet's Ecstasy' [Wisteriaic]. Then you have 'Sun Drop' [Chiven Lantern Plant]

* 'Light in Fairy Land' [Air Plant]
* 'Joy in Fairy Land' [Kleinhovia hospita]
* and 'Smile of Beauty' [Japanese Flowering Cherry]

Sometimes both the fruits and the flowers of a tree have a spiritual meaning and the relation is significant. The fruit of the 'Patience' flower is called 'Accomplishment'. The mango flower is 'Nature's hope for realisation' and the mango fruit is 'Divine Knowledge'. Grapes are 'Divine Ananda'.

In the pomegranate tree, the fully double red flower is 'Divine Love', the single one-layered red-petalled flower 'Divine Sacrifice', the fruit is 'Divine Love spreading over the world' and the white double flower is 'Unmanifest Divine Love'.

Humility *Adorable in its simplicity.*

Some wild flowers.

No.	Spiritual Name	Common name (India)	Common name (West)	Botanical name
1.	Artistic taste		Blue dawn flower	Ipomoea acuminata
2.	Courage	Mudar		Calotropis procera
3.	Gratitude			Ipomoea carnea
4.	Humility		Dropseed	Sporobolus capillaris
5.	Integral immortality		Globe amaranth	Gomphrena globosa
6.	Integral simplicity		Creeping daisy	Vittadinia
7.	Lightness		Jerusalem thorn	Parkinsonia aculeate
8.	Logic in thoughts		Mesquite	Prosopis glandulosa torreyiana
9.	Straightforwardness	Rukmini	Torch tree	Ixora arborea
10.	True worship			Lucas aspera
11.	Trust in the Divine			Asystasia coromandeliana
12.	Vital sensitivity	Chui-mui	Sensitive plant	Mimosa pudica

Flowers with interesting variations of size (smaller-detailed), of single and multiple petals (perfect), of multiple colours (manifold).

No. Spiritual Name	Description	Botanical name
1. a) Endurance	Sturdy compositae flower	Zinnia
b) Detailed endurance	Small single yellow, orange or white	
c) Manifold endurance	Variegated or multi-coloured	
2. a) Generosity	Single or double flowers with delicate recurved petals	Impatiens
b) Manifold Generosity	Multi-coloured	
3. a) Gratitude	Pale pinkish-white shaded	Ipomoea
b) Detailed gratitude	Small white flowers	
4. a) Mental purity	Single white salverform flower	Tabernaemontana coronaria
b) Perfect mental purity	Double fragrant white flower	
5. a) The New creation	Tubular waxy white flower	Polianthes tuberose
b) The Perfect new creation	Waxy double flower	
6. a) Plasticity	Double Composite flowers	Tagetes
b) Detailed plasticity	Dwarf varieties in all colours	
7. a) Protection	Clusters of showy bracts enclosing small flowers	Bougainvillea
b) Manifold protection	Clusters of two or more different coloured bracts	
8. a) Radiating purity	Single flowers	Gardenia jasminoides
b) Perfect radiating purity	Waxy white double flowers	
9. a) Receptivity	Elegant flared or ruffled tubular flowers	Gladiolus
b) Manifold receptivity	Multi-coloured shades	
10. a) Obedience	Single rotate flower	Dianthus
b) Perfect obedience	Double flower	
c) Detailed obedience	Clusters of small single fragrant rotate flowers	
11. a) Surrender	Highly fragrant pink roses	Rosa
b) Perfect surrender	Large double pink roses	
c) Detailed surrender	Tiny pink roses	
12. a) Quiet mind	Single white flowers	Nerium oleander
b) Perfect quietness in the mind	Double white flowers	

Flowers and their fruits both having spiritual names.

1. a) Mango flower is "Nature's hope for realisation"
   b) Mango fruit is "Divine Knowledge"
2. a) Bokul flower (Mimusops elengi) is "Patience"
   b) and its fruit is "Accomplishment"
3. a) Climbing Ylang-Ylang flower (Artabotrys odoratissimus) is "Clear Mind"
   b) and its fruit is "Reason"
4. a) Grapes are "Divine Ananda"
5. a) Pomegranate flower fully double is "Divine Love"
   b) Pomegranate flower single with one-layered petals is "Divine sacrifice"
   c) Pomegranate white flower is "Unmanifest Divine Love"
   d) Pomegranate fruit is "Divine Love spreading over the world".

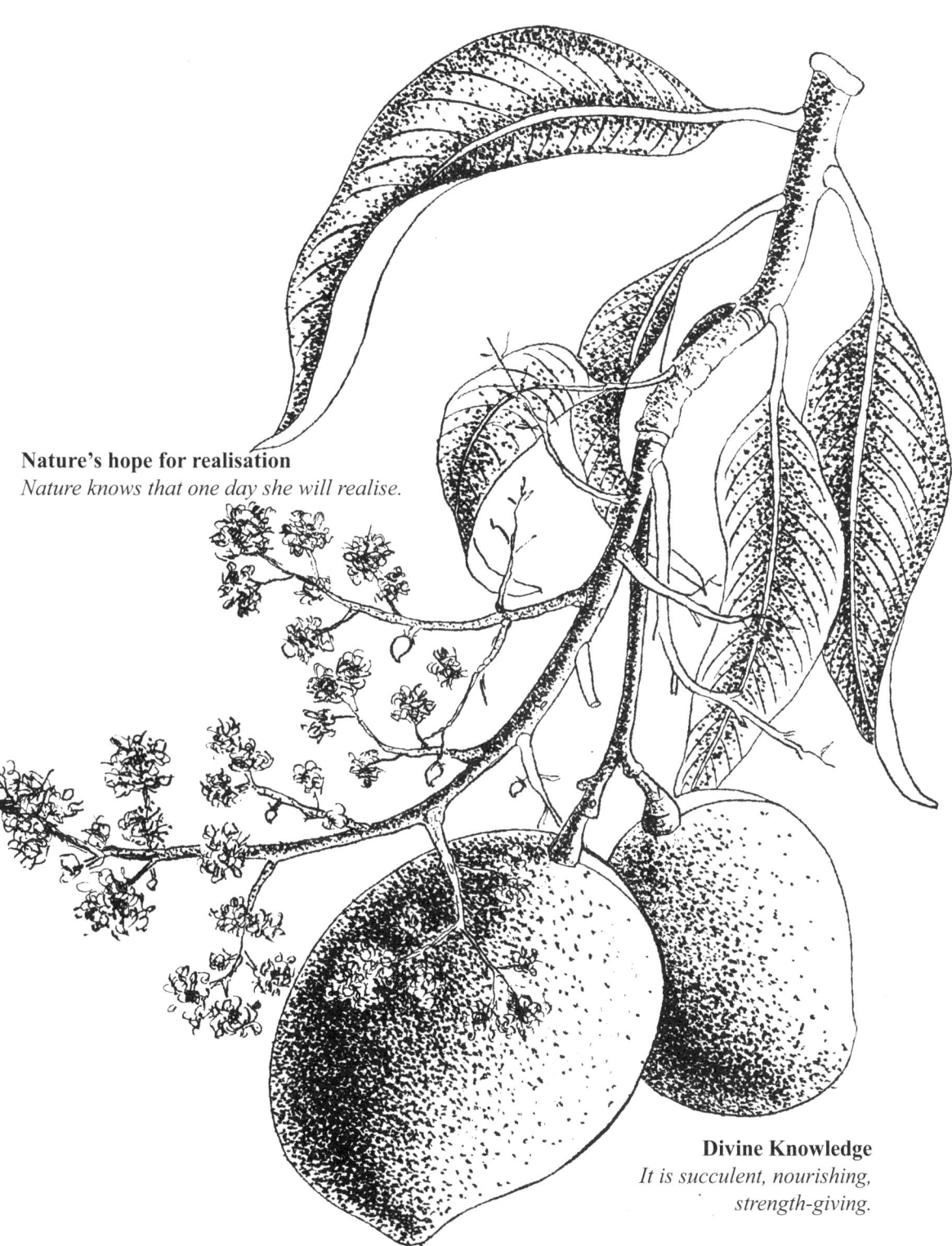

Nature's hope for realisation
Nature knows that one day she will realise.

Divine Knowledge
It is succulent, nourishing, strength-giving.

The Dahlia Series

No.	Spiritual Name	Description
1.	Vanity	Small single flowers with flat petals and hard centre, all colours.
2.	Pride	Small semi-double or double flowers, all colours.
3.	Dignity	Medium to fairly large double flowers, several colours.
4.	Nobility	Very large, dark red flowers.
5.	Aristocracy	Very large flowers in several colours often variegated.
6.	Superhumanity	Very large pure white flowers.

The Complementary Movement

Who or what are the demons? In India they are called the 'asuras', the brothers of the gods. They also are the manifestations of the one Divine, but have taken upon themselves his darker aspects so that they too may be transformed. Therefore, says Sri Aurobindo in one of his aphorisms, they are greater than even the gods.

So also with flowers. Most of them have a happy, beautiful and positive meaning. There are, though, a few which have names depicting the opposite and contrary qualities. They are the negative and complementary side of the same movement in Nature.

Here are a few interesting observations: 'Sharp tongue' looks like a sharp tongue. 'Boastfulness' imitates the Kadamba flower under whose tree Krishna played his magical flute. 'Gossip' has, significantly, a very bad smell!

We have flowers with such significances as 'Greed for Money', 'Passion', 'Vanity', 'Chatter', etc. How do these flowers represent a psychic prayer?

These flowers offer their bad vibrations for transformation.

Flowers with negative significances

No. Spiritual Name – (Botanical Name)

1. Boastfulness (Parkia biglandulosa)
2. Gossip (Typhonium)
3. Greed for money (Ochna serrulata)
4. Passion (Spathodea campanulata)
5. Pride (Dahlia – small semi-double or doubled)
6. Sharp tongue (Aphelandra tetragona)
7. Vanity (Dahlia – small, single petal with hard centre)

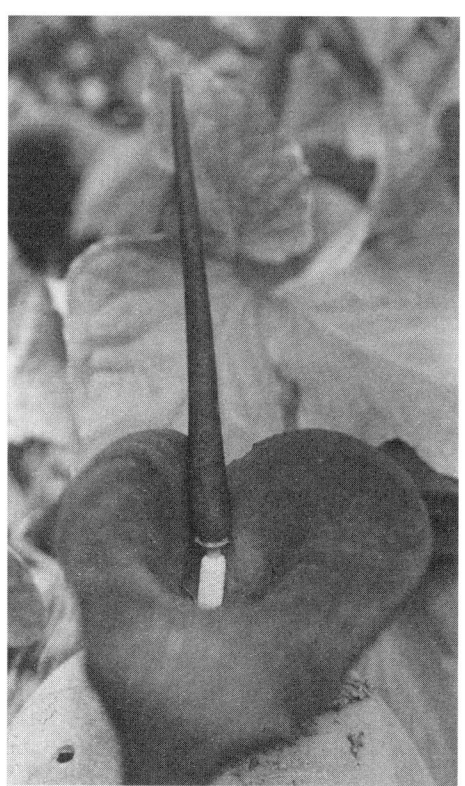

Gossip
Dark and pointed, this flower hurts more than it charms.

Interesting Names and Uses

The Divine, undoubtedly, has a sense of humour. But his humour, like all things, contains a deeper truth. Here we recount the names given by the Mother to the flowers of some herbs and plants we eat or use in our everyday life.

The little bitter gourd, Karela, is named 'Sweetness'. The Chilly is 'A Whipping', the Coconut flower is 'Multitude' and the Pumpkin flower is 'Abundance'. The Saunph flower is 'Light in the blood' and the Drumstick flower is 'Hygienic organisation'.

The aspiration and quality of the flowers are not necessarily passed on to the fruits. Otherwise, the Coffee flower could not have been called the 'Perfect Path' or the Betelnut flower, 'Steadfast Vitality' or the Tobacco flower, 'Common Sense'.

Multitude   *Gives itself without stint and satisfies innumerable needs.*

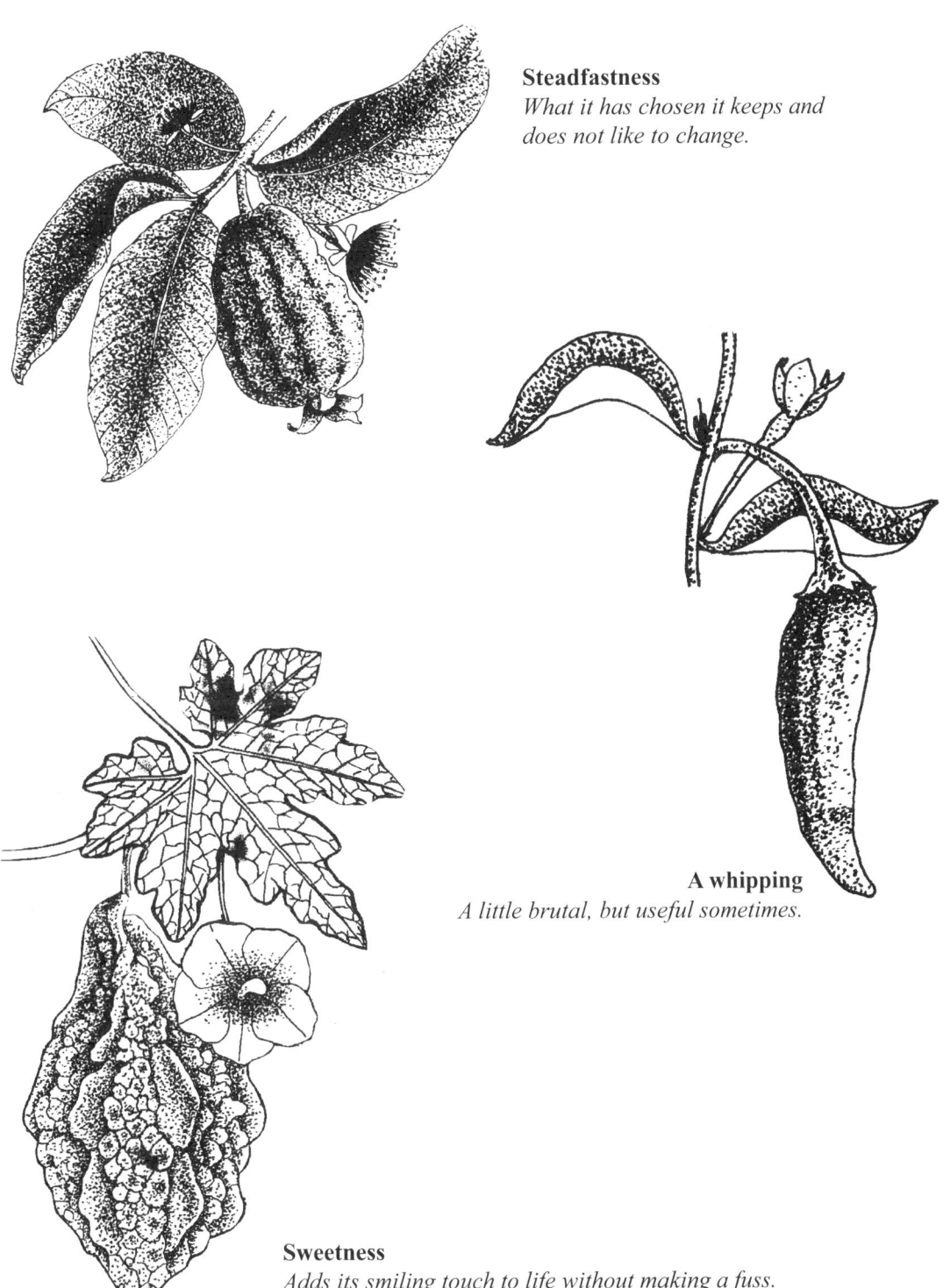

Steadfastness
What it has chosen it keeps and does not like to change.

A whipping
A little brutal, but useful sometimes.

Sweetness
Adds its smiling touch to life without making a fuss.

Flowers and plants we use in our daily lives in various forms – vegetables, fruits, roots, seeds, leaves, bark, wood etc.

No.	Common name (India)	Common name (West)	Spiritual name	Botanical name
1.	Karela	Bitter gourd	Sweetness	Momordca charantia
2.	Brinjal	Eggplant	Fearlessness in the vital	Solanum melongena
3.	Kumara	Pumpkin	Abundance	Cucurbita maxima
4.	Sahijan	Drum stick	Hygienic organisation	Moringa oleifera
5.	Mirchi	Chilly	A whipping	Capsicum annuum
6.	Bok		Beginning of Realisation	Sesbania grandiflora
7.	Nimbu	Lemon	Chastity	Citrus lemonia
8.	Nariyal	Coconut	Multitude	Cocos nucifera
9.	Bijora	Grape fruit	Continence	Citrus grandis
10.	Amrud	Guava	Steadfastness	Psidium guajava
11.	Bael		Devotional attitude	Aegle marmelos
12.	Jamun	Rose apple	Mastery	Syzygium jambos
13.	Kamarakh	Carambola	Organised teamwork	Averrhoa carambola
14.		Japanese cherry	Smile of beauty	Prunus serrulata
15.		Singapore cherry	Primitive succulence	Muntingia calabura
16.	Dhaniya	Coriander	Delicacy	Coriandrum sativum
17.	Neem	Margosa	Spiritual atmosphere	Azadirachta indica
18.	Mahaneem	Persian lilac	Distinction of the vital	Melia azedarach
19.	Mehndi	Hennah	Energy turned towards the Divine	Lawsonia inermis
20.		Lemon grass	Help	Cymbopogon
21.	Tambakhoo	Tobacco	Common sense	Nicotiana alata "grandiflora"
22.	Haldi	Turmeric	Peace	Curcuma
23.	Badam	Almond	Smile of Nature	Prunus communis
24.	Ilaichi	Cardamom	To know what is to be said	Alpinia galangal
25.	Supari	Betel nut	Steadfast vitality	Areca catechu
26.	Saunph	Fennel	Light in the blood	Foeniculum vulgare
27.	Coffee	Coffee	The perfect path	Coffea species
28.	Til	Sesame	Conciliation	Sesamum indicum
29.		Poppy	Spontaneous joy of nature	Papaver rhoeas
30.		Teak	Renunciation of desires	Tectona grandis
31.		Eucalyptus	Abolition of the ego	Eucalyptus
32.	Rui	Cotton (yellow or white with red centre)	Material abundance	Gossypium
33.		Silk cotton	Success in the most material vital	Gossypium arboreum
34.		Yellow silk cotton	Success in supramental works	Cochlospermum religiosa
35.		Red silk cotton	Solid steadfastness in the material consciousness	Bombax malabaricum
36.		White silk cotton	Material enterprises	Ceiba pentanbra

Clock of Nature

Life moves in a cycle. Nature too, but in her more precise orderly way. There are flowers which bloom only once at fixed times of the year, and there are others which blossom only at particular times of the day – the flower-clocks and flower-calendars of Nature.

There is obviously an occult significance behind these phenomena – things which cannot be easily explained or categorised. In the flower-clock, especially, there can be a great variation in time, due to the weather, the place, the condition of the plant and, as we shall see later, even the gardener.

Mother, certain flowers come in a particular season; does this mean that during that season a greater force is at work?

If one is quite attentive, one will see that in different seasons one flower is replaced by another with a similar or close significance, and you can go all round the year in this way – if you know how to make use of things! There are also permanent things which are always there…. But flowers, for example, like the "transformation" flowers, have a season, quite a long one, but still a season. The "realisation" flower has a fairly long season, but it doesn't come at the same time as the "transformation" flower…. They… how shall I put it?... overlap. One begins before the other finishes. But the seasons when they come abundantly are not the same, and all flowers are like that. Yes, it is arranged. This answers your question, doesn't it? These are shades in the meaning and it is possible that some seasons are more favourable; one may lay greater stress on one movement than on another.

THE MOTHER

Flowers in the Clock of Nature*

No.	Spiritual Name	Common name (India)	Common name (West)	Botanical name
	Midnight & after			
1.	Complexity of the centres		Canna	Canna
2.	Friendship with the Divine		Indian Shot	Canna indica
	Very early morn			
3.	Divine Grace	Gul-i-Ajaib	Changeable Rose	Hibiscus mutabilis
4.	Service	Iyavakai	Copper-pod	Peltaphorum pterocarpum
	Pre-dawn			
5.	Realisation	Gul Mohur	Flamboyant	Delonix regia
6.	Quiet mind	Kanel	Sweet-scented oleander	Nerium oleander
7.	Opening of the material vital to the light			Thunbergia erecta

* These times vary with the seasons, the length of the day and the influence of cloudy days.

After sunrise
8. Charity — Day flower — Commelina species
9. Eternal youth — — Hibiscus miniatus
10. Dynamic power — — Hibiscus
11. Light of the purified power — — Hibiscus
12. Awakening of the physical mind — — Turnera ulmifolia elegans
13. Movements in the light — — Pentas

Midmorning
13. Aspiration in the physical for the supramental light — Rukmini rangan — Ixora — Ixora singaporensis
14. Silence — Kaurav Pandav — Blue passion flower — Passiflora caerulea
15. Sri Aurobindo's compassion — — Rose Moss — Portulaca grandiflora
16. Beauty of supramental love — — — Hibiscus
17. Devotion — Tulsi — Sacred basil — Ocimum sanctum

Late morning
19. Beauty of the New Creation — — — 'Hawaiian' hibiscus

Noon & after
20. Integral gratitude — — — Operculina turpethum
21. Psychological perfection — Champaka — Temple tree — Plumeria

Afternoon
22. Vital fantasy — — Fame Flower — Talinum patens
23. Humility before the Divine in the physical nature — — — Pavitta thomsonii

Before evening
24. The New Creation — Rajanigandha — Tuberose — Polianthes tuberose
25. Enthusiasm — — Petunia — Petunia hybrida
26. Solace — — 4 o'clock flower — Mirabilis jalapa

Sunset & after
27. Satchidananda — Dulaba champa — Ginger-lily — Hedychium
28. Purity — Juhi — Jasmina — Jasminum
29. Occultism — — — Pancratium littoralis
30. Transformation — — — Millingtonia hortensis
31. Joy of spirituality — — Bowstring hemp — Sansevieria grandis
32. Air — Raat-ki-Rani — Night queen — Cestrum nocturnum
33. Faithfulness — Madhumalti — Rangoon creeper — Quisqualis indica

Late evening
34. Integral wealth of Mahalaxmi — — Water lily — Nymphaea
35. Supramental riches — — Large cactus flower — Selenicereus

Before midnight
36. Fire — Krishnachuda — Peacock flower — Poinciana pulcherrima
37. Fortune — — Hedge cactus — Cereus
38. Beauty in collective simplicity — — Star of Bethlehem — Ornithogalum umbellatum
39. Gratitude — — — Ipomea

Exceptions to the rule: Krishna's Ananda (no fixed time, usually day-time)
Power of truth in the Subconscient: early morning or anytime during the day.

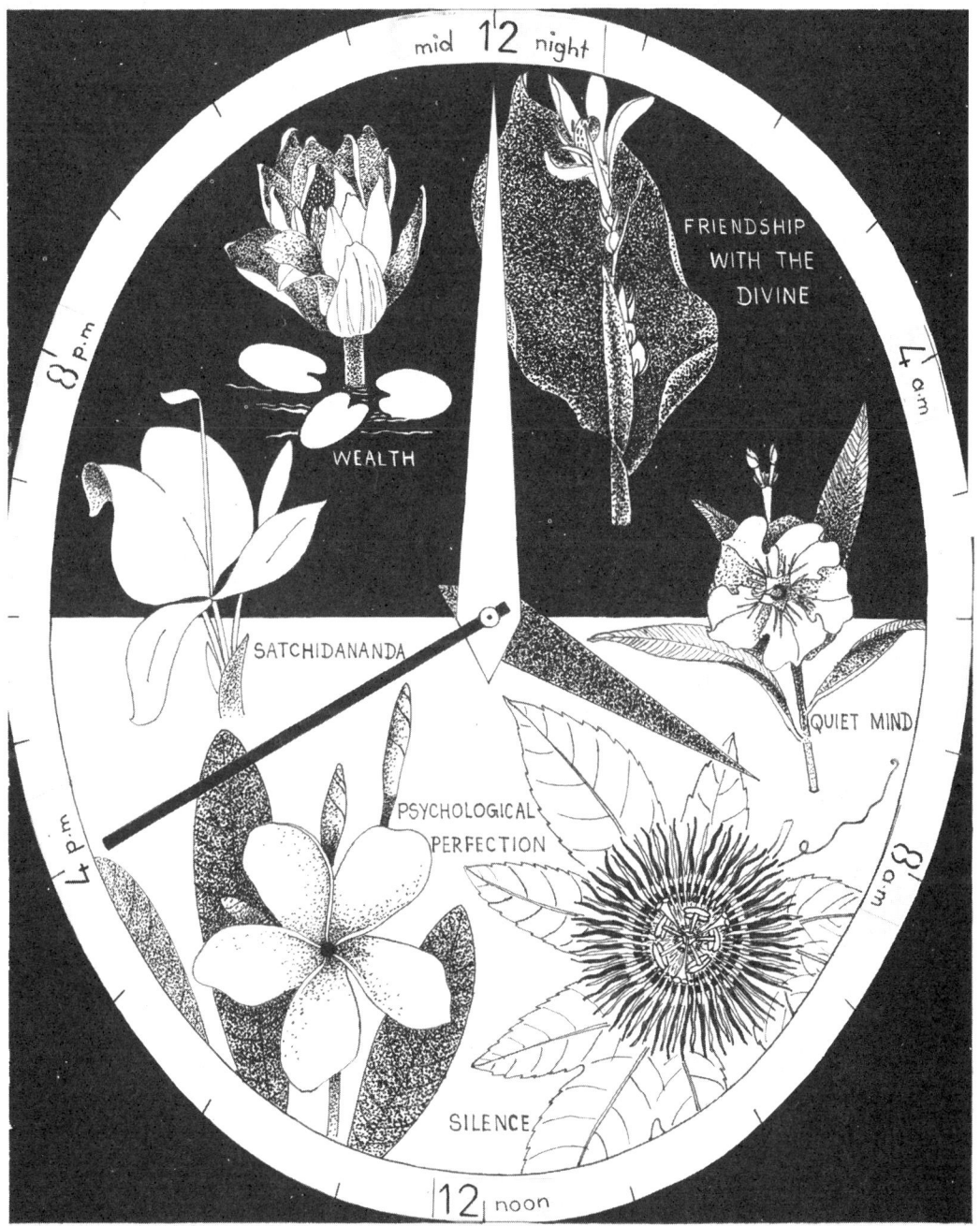

The Wonderland of Flowers

In this book we have laid stress on the spiritual aspect of flowers. But even if we look at them botanically and scientifically we can only marvel at their beauty and mystery.

There are in the plant kingdom over 2,65,000 different kinds of plants and each one of them has millions of their own kind. But man's attraction has been for flowering plants. We have amongst us over 1,50,000 species of plants which have flowers. Of these only about 3000 plants are specially cultivated for their attractive flowers.

There is in nature a profusion in the kind, colour, smell, size and variety of flowers. The mottled orange-brown and white parasitic stinking corpse lily (Rafflesia Arnoldi) has the largest of blooms. These attach themselves to the cissus vines in the jungles of East Asia. They are up to three feet in diameter and attain a weight of fifteen pounds. The stalk and spadix of the massive green and purple flowers of Amerphophalus in Sumatra, attains a length of five feet. I have myself seen the Sausage tree give flowers in profusion in 2 metre racemes. They have a strong scent too. The flowers rising from the tips of branches go on growing reaching the ground. Though generally flowers are borne on the tips of branches, there are a few trees that bear flowers on their main trunk and none on their branches. Prosperity (Couroupita) is one of such plants whose beautiful flowers cluster around the main stem. There are some plants whose flowers you can see only with the help of a lens. For example the world's smallest flower can be seen floating in ponds in blankets of light green colour. Each plant you can hold on the tip of your fingers. But remember, this plant and its flowers were there long before you came on the scene in evolutionary history.

One of the earliest of flowers is the sacred Lotus. Scientists are also agreed that basically all other flowers evolved from the flowers of this family. It is a primitive flower, they say, because it does not care for economy, that is, it has a large number of parts, showy and fragrant. As flowers evolved the number of parts and their size got reduced. They became more efficient and the height of efficiency is achieved in the flowers of grass. Yet they have a beauty and humility all their own.

While on one side, for the sake of efficiency,

Prosperity
Stays consistently only with him who offers it to the Divine.

some plants reduced the size of flowers, others decided that the best way was for hundreds of flowers to get together and work in union to achieve the same result. We have this efficiency in the sunflower. If you observe carefully, you will see hundreds of separate flowers closely packed in the dense centre. The sunflower is, in fact, a bunch of flowers.

Then we have a bizarre group of flowers. There are about 500 species of these which attract animals – chiefly insects, only to eat them and digest them – the carnivorous plants.

Rarely does nature produce flowers that last a long time. Some flowers bloom only for a few hours. Some do not open unless the sun is bright. There are others which last a long time — like orchid flowers. They can last for weeks. There is a flower which lasts months and months. It looks like a chrysanthemum and is called the Ever Lasting Flower.

Some flowers you can see only once in the lifetime of a plant. You have to wait decades to see the Bamboo flowers or the flowers of some species of Agave. The effort for producing flowers is so exhausting that the plants die after the flowers mature. The phenomenon of Bamboo flowering in the forest is very impressive and there is an aroma for miles and miles around. But alas the whole Bamboo forest dies. To clear the debris, so to say, armies of rats descend from nowhere and eat up the vast quantities of seeds to keep the balance of nature!

The arrangement of flowers on a plant seems to follow some occult pattern. If you try to trace the form of a flower you will find harmonious patterns emerging from them like force fields. They seem to merge and emerge again and again.

The world of flowers is a world by itself. Enter into it and you will be happy to discover at each moment the unexpected thrill of Nature.

DAYANAND

To create a little flower is the labour of ages.

William Blake

Attachment to the Divine
Wraps itself around the Divine and finds all its support in Him so as to be sure never to leave Him.

A Play of Nature

How interesting it is to notice the similarities between different mechanisms in Nature. It is as though all science and skill were the creation and play of one mastermind. The plant growing in the field and the industrial complex in full activity have so much in common. The mysteries of a detective story may grip certain readers but the mysteries of Nature and her infinite tricks, ruses, detours, feints, nay even practical jokes may be more absorbing for one who reads the book of Nature.

We will limit ourselves here to the process of reproduction – by what subtle ruses and subterfuges, it may seem, does Nature combine the characters of two distinct individuals without however destroying the characteristics of the parent plants nor blindly leaping forward without rhyme or reason – a step by step process as intricate as a game of chess!

We will not study how a plant seed is formed by the union of a pollen grain and an ovule – an experiment more intricate than the production of nuclear energy. We are going to observe by what contrivance some of the myriad varieties of plants manage to simply make sure that the pollen reaches the stigma of a flower of the same kind. And this too from observations not made by experts and specialists but by what even poets and simple men have seen and reasoned out. Is not this too one of Nature's ways of having fun!

In the earlier stages of evolution, the most natural vehicle for the transportation of pollen was the wind. Therefore the first flowers upon earth were the "anemophiles". In the coniferous plants the pollen are like balloons of hot air. With the sun, the air contained in the sac of the pollen heats and expands and the balloon floats and rises in the air. In the shade or at night, the air in the balloon cools, and the pollen descends becoming smaller and heavier. But to fulfil its function it must land on a stigma and the chances of this happening are not very great. Nature's answer is that myriads of balloons are launched into the air. During the spring, in some favourable years the yellow green dust of pollen from the pine trees enters houses in large quantities like fine sand. One inflorescence of Maize can liberate 50 million grains of pollen. And there can be as many as 30,000 plants to a field.

It has been found that the Ragweed alone liberates one million tons of pollen over North America every year. If we now add all the pollen spread by all the plants over the entire earth, this dust could, in quantity, replace all the cement used by men to construct houses, roads and bridges! Yet how many of these grains of pollen actually land on the stigma of a flower of the same kind? Here is another example of the characteristic and frequent largeness of Nature, which we with our human criteria call the mighty wastage of Nature.

But Nature has also other and more efficient ways. This was made possible with the coming of the insects, millions of years ago. The role of insects in the fecundation of plants was discovered by Sprengel, the director of a school at Spandau, near Berlin. He had the habit of wandering in the fields on Sundays and wrote a book of his observations. The response was so hostile that the publishers of the now famous book, which is looked upon as a classic, even refused to give Sprengel the copies due to the author. And the school authorities seeing that Sprengel, instead of going to church on Sundays, was spending his days in the fields were furious. Sprengel was censured and removed for negligence of duties and compelled to live in poverty. It was only much later that

Darwin stumbled upon the book. Typically the teacher, prosecuted and ridiculed during his lifetime, became after his death, the glory of his native place.

Sprengel discovered that Nature had found a very ingenious answer to a difficult problem. Instead of the wind the insects performed the function of carrying pollen from one plant to another. For this the insect had first to be attracted to a flower by its bright colours and pleasing fragrance. Inside the flower was the precious pollen, but the insect instead of eating this was led to take something much cheaper – sweet water or nectar. On its way it had to deposit the pollen it had brought from a previous flower exactly on the stigma. While leaving it had to carry, unknowingly, new pollen for depositing on the next flower.

The first problem, therefore, that the flower has to solve in this intriguing play is to make the right choice among the various visitors. It is obvious that an automotive mechanism which will work with a bumble bee cannot be put into action by a fly and similarly a night-moth cannot play the role of a bee. Fig.1 shows different flowers suitable for bees, bumble-bees, moths and butterflies.

When the red clover was introduced in Australia it grew well but could not reproduce itself. Finally suitable bumble-bees had to be released before the plant could multiply. There are certain flowers which float so freely in air and whose nectar is hidden so deep inside the long corolla that they can be reached only by the humming-bird. They flutter over the flowers like helicopters. "For humming-birds only" announces the flower as it powders the back of the bird with pollen from its stamens while the humming-bird flutters and sucks the nectar from deep within the corolla (Fig.2).

This symbiosis between particular plants, birds and insects is a most fascinating play of Nature. Snapdragons are closed with a trap so

heavy that only the big bumble-bees can lift them. The balls of Fuchsia can be reached only by extremely dextrous insects like the bees. Only a visitor as intelligent and as tenacious as the honey bee will enter sufficiently deep inside the flower of the Sage and press its head sufficiently against the filament of the stamen so that, like the keys of a typewriter, the stamen will strike it on the back, and print in bright gold with pollen the inscription "has visited the Sage flowers" (Fig. 3).

The bees are blind to red, while violet excites them and their favourite colour is yellow. Landing on a flower the insect follows the many-coloured lines which lead it towards the nectar inside. When the flower of the chestnut-tree opens it is pale yellow. As it matures the yellow turns to bright orange. Only

then does the bee enter into the flower. Once it is fertilised the 'lines of nectar' change their colour and become purple. The bees that come now simply turn back without entering.

Nature is full of great variety and ingenuity. One of the most magnificent creations of Nature is the Orchid. It grows as a parasite on trees. Its carrier is the bumble-bee and the way it deals with it is unique. The bumble-bee has merely to sit on the pink "stool" at the entrance and out comes a sumptuous plate from the automatic restaurant inside. This is due to the weight of the bumble-bee which activates a lever to bring out a plate in the form of a beautiful shell full of a tasty creamy substance. Having finished its meal, the bumble-bee lifts its head which rubs along the inner part of the flower and knocks against the white painted sign board of the restaurant. A sharp point in the board fixes itself behind the head of the bumble-bee, which, while trying to extricate itself, tears away the whole signboard and carries the malicious gift of the flower, like the barbs in the neck of the bull in the arena. Carrying this point with two sacs of pollen on its upper extremity the insect flies away. These two sacs, which were balancing on the head of the insect like a plume slowly curve forward and come in front of the eyes of the bumble bee like a pair of spectacles. Already a new orchid presents itself and, in spite of its disagreeable earlier experience, the insect cannot resist its temptation. It settles on the pink stool, and by magic a new tasty plate appears. The bee plunges its head to lick and the pollen is very precisely deposited on the stigma waiting there behind the plate. The sacs of pollen get detached to give place to a new set of barbs which will implant themselves on the insect when it leaves the flower like a flying bull. Thus from flower to flower our bee is successively and successfully harpooned or relieved of its harpoons (Fig.4).

Indeed Nature has its own sense of drama and humour. There is no doubt that the flowers attract insects with their shape, their colour and their fragrance. But there are too many mysteries and exceptions which make us hesitate from giving a simple and purely rational explanation. Some flowers attract insects and others don't. Yet the latter are in no way any worse off. Some flowers are fragrant and others not and yet these are as much visited by insects as the others. One does not always see the advantage of the presence of these characteristics or the disadvantage of their absence. Why all this? Of what use is a rule, when the exceptions are so many that one does not know whether the rule is the exception or vice versa?

One can only wonder at the beauty and mystery and infinite variety of Nature.

(Based on "The Book of Nature" by Dr. F. Kahn)

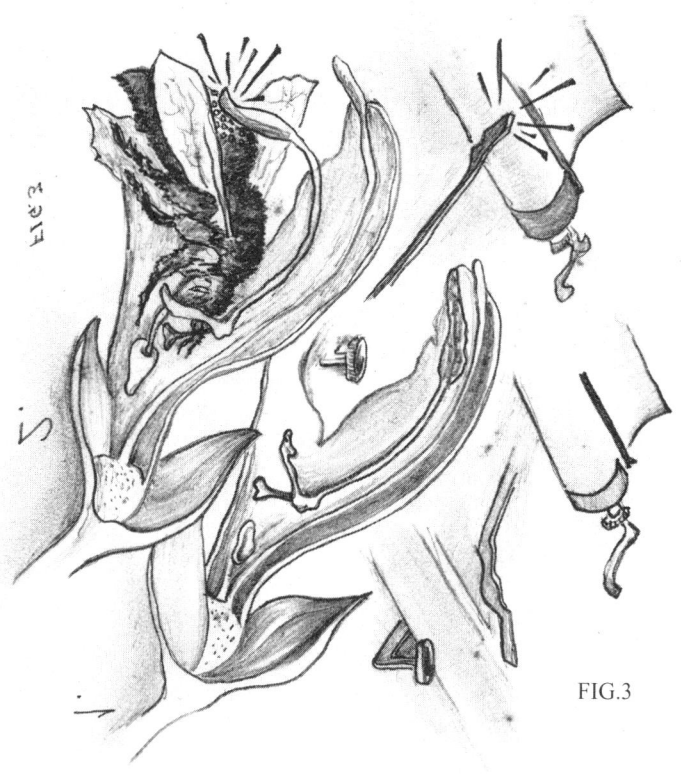

FIG.3

FIG. 4

Happy Companions

We can communicate with flowers, we can speak to them, listen to them. They can be happy companions at all times. They respond to our love and affection by growing better and even blooming exactly when we want them most to do so. Most gardeners and many children know this. But it is a truth we can all experience.

Flowers speak to us when we know how to listen to them – it is a subtle and fragrant language.

*

Innumerable like ideas, flowers are joyous companions.

*

Flowers are very receptive and they are happy when they are loved.

*

What is the way to get out of the obsession of pain when it is too much?

Look at a beautiful flower.

*

It is quite certain, for instance, that if you have a special affection for a plant, if, in addition to the material care you give it, you love it, if you feel close to it, it feels this; its blossoming is much more harmonious and happy, it grows better, it lives longer. All this means a response in the plant itself. Consequently, there is the presence there of a certain consciousness; and surely the plant has a vital being.

*

Plants have feeling, they are alive, they should not be treated brutally.

As a rule plants suffer if they are kept shut up in a room.

*

There are many plants we are trying to grow here which suffer because of our climate. How can we help them to grow and blossom here?

Naturally, plants which like cold climates would grow in greenhouses. Also by planting forests one could have a regulating action on the climate.

Growth of consciousness in the atmosphere will surely have an effect which it is difficult to describe beforehand.

*

Why do plants fall ill and what can we do to help them?

When man does not meddle, the illness of plants seems to be accidental. But man's action has upset the life of plants, even as that of animals, of course.

Men have upset the life of plants and animals, and supermen have upset the life of men.

How to develop our consciousness in order to work in a better way with plants and flowers?

First you must learn to be silent, then note carefully what happens in the consciousness.

*

What is the best way of opening ourselves to the deep influence of flowers?

To love them. If you can enter into psychic contact with them, then that would be perfect.

*

Love of flowers is a valuable help for finding and uniting with the psychic.

*

By communing with flowers, we can see that the vegetal kingdom already has her own way of aspiring towards the Divine.

THE MOTHER

Thou hast put into these flowers magical virtue: they seem to speak of Thy sole Presence; they bring with them the smile of the Divine.

The Mother

The Mother's Ways with Flowers

The Mother had her own way with flowers. In the midst of her heavy schedule and pressing engagements, She would find time to arrange a vase, apparently oblivious to everything else. Here are the reminiscences of a few persons who had the privilege of coming close to the Mother or communing with her through flowers.

Experiences with Plants

The Mother has given spiritual significances to flowers and one must have some identity with flowers to really understand what a flower represents. It is a subjective experience which is difficult to objectivise, though people having the same consciousness can share their experience.

The Mother did not always give a significance immediately when a flower was offered to her. For, we must remember that flowers were blessings and a flower had to have an inner meaning in the growth of the consciousness and in the sadhana of the seeker. She was mostly concerned with the flowers we were ourselves growing here for they formed part of our life and field of growth.

I would like to recount some anecdotes of the Mother's ways with flowers.

Once when the Mother was visiting the Lake and was being shown the progress made, she had to cross a field where wild flowers were growing. She stopped, before proceeding, at the edge of the field studded with tiny blossoms of all sorts of wild flowers. She asked with a smile, "But where can I put my foot?" And yet the same Mother could, with the same love, also pull off sprigs of Harmony from a large flowering branch in joy and appreciation of our collective effort in presenting her play *Ascent to the Truth*. She was indeed the Mother and each of her movements fitted a divine plan.

There is a little yellow flower that blooms on the most dainty looking small tree you ever saw. The thin narrow leaves have tiny leaflets all along both sides and all the leaves together wave and sway in the slightest breeze giving a joyous dancing movement to the slender branches.

Now our head gardener – who regularly took flowers to the Mother and could bring a new flower to her at nearly any time – was surprised when she remained silent when he brought that flower to her.

Several years passed by and then one day a young lady quite spontaneously took a large flowering branch to the Mother. After a pause the Mother said to her: "Oh! This is Lightness!" Our gardener friend was delighted to hear of the new name and must have wondered why the Mother never told him that! Well the divine logic becomes a little more clear when we realise that this woman was a dancer and it was on her birthday that she offered this flower to the Mother.

I had a similar experience with a particular flower growing on a thorny tree. It is called the Coral Tree and has bright red attractive flowers that bloom at the end of the branches. Usually there are no leaves when the tree is in bloom. This tree becomes, in early spring, a true landmark, or, for me, a beacon towards which I must go, attracted as irresistibly as a moth to the light. It was impossible to climb the tree though numerous birds could enjoy the nectar perching on the highest branches. I would pick up any complete flower knocked unwittingly down by the more clumsy birds and carefully take away my treasure.

When I showed this flower to my gardener friend he laughed and said that he remembered seeing a sadhak bringing these flowers to the Mother on a conspicuous branch. Before he could come near she vehemently told him not to bring those flowers to her. She could not even stand their presence! Either then or later she gave some bad meaning to them. I have quite forgotten.

So I wrote to the Mother telling her that I was very attracted to this flower although I had been told she did not like it. She accepted the loose flowers I had sent through a sadhak who took my note to read to her and she asked him to give her a piece of paper on which she wrote in French, "Beginning of realisation in Matter"! This he brought to me and the name filled me with joy and intense aspiration to identify myself with this flower and its deep power of fulfilment.

It seems to me that the consciousness of the person presenting the flowers had also a role in determining the spiritual significance of the flowers.

The Mother herself always got a beautiful response from the plants. Once she gave a sprig of Divine Love to a sadhak, who was one of the Ashram gardeners, with the request: "Can we grow this? He thought for a moment and then said: "Yes, Mother."

The sprig was planted, but nothing seemed to be growing and he had some misgivings. However, he was informed that the Mother took keen interest in the little sprig. When the Mother came to know his despair, she asked that the small pot containing that sprig be brought and kept in a place where she could see it every

Lightness
Charming but at times thorny.

day. It was done and the Mother looked at it every time she passed by.

A few days later, new buds were seen and the small cutting grew vigorously. The Mother asked to transplant it into a bigger pot since the roots filled up the small pot. It filled one pot after another. Finally, it was suggested that it could be planted in the Ashram rockery, where you now see it as a full grown shrub or a little tree.

I believe a friendly understanding of the basic needs of vegetal life is necessary for establishing a contact with plants. Surprisingly, one of the most important needs of a plant is the same as that of a child: to be loved and recognised. The Mother says somewhere that a young child is so small that its chief need is to make itself seen or heard. Taking this hint, I often put my best plant of the day or week "on the throne" where it can be seen and admired.

Beginning of realisation in matter
Matter responds to the divine influence.

I have also observed that special flowers bloom on special days, such as darshan days or birthdays in response to the consciousness or aspiration of the person concerned. For example, this year in my garden, Agni and Sri Aurobindo's compassion bloomed on Sri Aurobindo's birthday. Sri Krishna's Ananda was in full bloom on Krishna's birthday. The Divine's Presence, the Divine's Help and the Light of the Purified Power bloom throughout the year in our garden. I had also observed some seasonal flowers blooming like perennials – Constant Remembrance of the Divine (Honeysuckle) and Attachment to the Divine (Ground Orchid Spathofluttis).

Flowers can indeed not only reflect our states of consciousness but also help to raise them higher.

RICHARD

Flowers and states of Consciousness

The relationship of a person to flowers depends on his state of consciousness. As the Mother used to say – it is difficult for persons to keep the flowers of gratitude fresh – for gratitude is a rare quality and quickly vanishes. I remember taking great care to take the flowers of Gratitude to the Mother. After plucking them carefully in the morning, keeping them in water, I used to wrap them in a wet cloth and wait at the Mother's door. When I was called inside I would unwrap the flowers most carefully to place them in the hands of the Mother. Those were delightful moments!

Generally I used to take only two flowers to the Mother for we formulated our prayer precisely through flowers – the Divine Presence and Realisation. Though Divine Presence blossoms round the year, one had to search for Realisation when it was off season. I grew my Divine Presence in a pot on the balcony. Somehow the plant seemed to know that every Sunday I would go to the Mother for Pranam, for invariably it presented me with the best bunch of flowers on one stalk on that day. The Mother used to be always surprised at the size and number of flowers on one stalk. This plant continued to give me these flowers week after week till May 20, 1973 on which day I had the great good fortune to do pranam to the Mother. After that somehow the flowers returned to the normal size and quantity, for I did never get an occasion for pranam again.

Those were precious eternal moments when the Mother took me far and deep into a timeless era.

But one day there was a surprise in store for me. Rather a shock. As usual I had placed the flowers in her hands and got lost. When I came back, I heard her calling Champaklalji who was ever present near her. She asked him for the flower Sincerity.

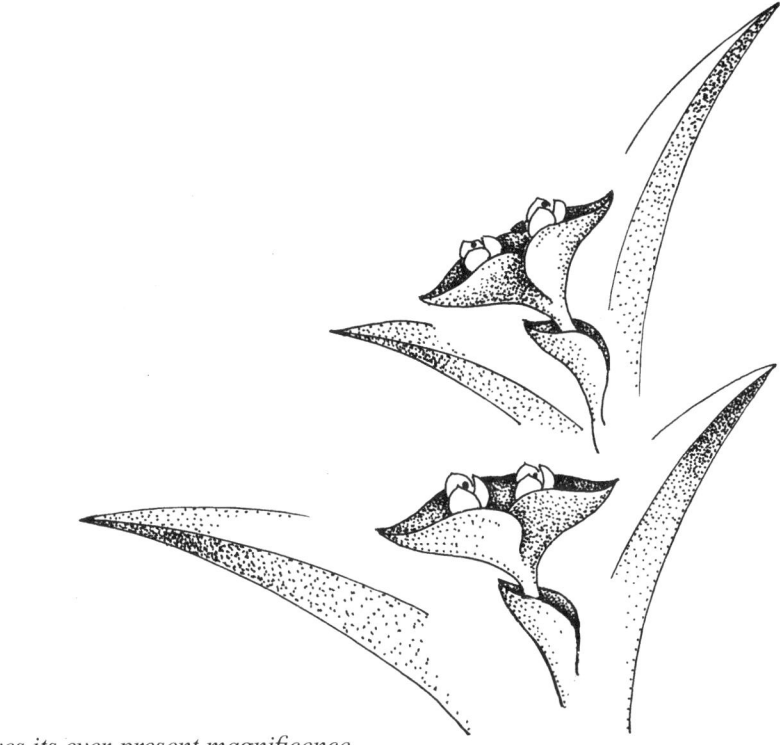

Divine presence
It hides from ignorant eyes its ever-present magnificence.

Normally She used to have these flowers around her chair but that day search as much as you like, Sincerity was not to be found. That was like a bolt from the blue. It awakened me. For without sincerity what can you realise!

DAYANAND

Communion with Flowers

The Mother once said that the pure psychic consciousness is instinctive to flowers. They are not only extremely receptive to the force put into them, but they transmit it too. Further on, she explained that flowers can answer and vibrate to the contact or the projection and accept the meaning.

The Mother granted me the privilege of communion with her through the flowers which conveyed my aspiration. And she sent back the container with her response.

I had a plant of country roses – Perfect Surrender – in a pot on my terrace near the sea. I was told that, generally speaking, roses do not like the salty sea breeze. But my plant seemed to be inwardly fortified enough to resist its adverse effect and grew normally.

My birthday was approaching and my intense aspiration was to realise perfect surrender. Well, believe it or not, on my birthday that lovely, friendly plant offered 23 roses on one single shoot, 18 on another and 11 on the third – all in clusters, whereas normally one sees five or seven roses at the most on one shoot of a branch. I was overwhelmed by this identity of consciousness in my plant, and its abundantly generous offering.

And to prove beyond any shadow of doubt how responsive plants can be to our consciousness, I had another miracle to its credit.

I was aspiring for an absolute integral love for the Divine and pure surrender. Lo! for my birthday, the flowers of the rose plant changed their colour from the usual pink to white, which is the colour of 'integral'.

For me, that was the delight of all delights. For, it was an assurance of the Mother's force helping my sadhana and the concrete proof that flowers respond to the projection of our consciousness.

I will give one more example. Once I observed that when my whole emphasis and concentration was on Truth, we happened to go to a friend's home where there was a plant which the Mother had named 'Effort towards the Truth'. This plant was sick. Its buds used to fall away before flowering. I silently told the plant that I wanted a flower for my birthday. And on my birthday, our friend brought me its first flower to be offered to the Mother – without knowing that I wanted this flower.

I will end this with a very amusing but a very typical comment by the Mother. Once I offered two lotuses to the Mother. One was a red lotus, absolutely straight and the other a white lotus a little curved downward. I felt sorry that it looked a bit drooping. The Mother must have caught my feeling. She held them in her hands for some time with concentration and said with a smile, "You know, it is exactly like Sri Aurobindo and me. He is looking upward with his gaze fixed high, whereas I am looking down, always concerned with this earth, and its condition."

KAILAS

Effort towards the Truth
Should exist in every man of goodwill.

Spirit of a Bamboo

I wish you, Friend,
That finest thing
That I can wish for you –
Not health, nor wealth,
Nor luck, but just
A spirit of bamboo.

    Bend with the wind
    And thus survive
    Though storms may flatten you.
    Weep not at fate,
    But spring erect
    As bamboo thickets do.

Wealth may be lost,
And health may fade,
Yet you'll be wise and true
If you can bend
And you can grow
With a spirit of bamboo!

Helen B. Grouse

Flowers speak to us

This is an excerpt from a beautiful and a very humorous book – 'My Family and Other Animals' by Gerald Durrell. Do flowers speak and actually behave in this manner? Can this be true? It is for us to find out.

The room was a forest of flowers; vases, bowls, and pots were perched everywhere, and each contained a mass of beautiful blooms that shone in the gloom, like walls of jewels in a green-shadowed cave....

Mrs. Kralefsky turned her head and smiled at me.

'They say', she announced – 'they *say* that when you get old, as I am, your body slows down. I don't believe it. No, I think that is quite wrong. I have a theory that you do *not slow down at all, but that life slows down for you.* You understand me? Everything becomes languid, as it were, and you can notice so much more when things are in slow motion. The things you see! The things you see! The extraordinary things that happen all around you, that you never even suspected before! It is really a delightful adventure, quite delightful!'

She sighed with satisfaction, and glanced round the room.

'Take flowers,' she said, pointing at the blooms that filled the room. 'Have you heard flowers *talking*?'

Greatly intrigued, I shook my head; the idea of flowers talking was quite new to me.

'Well I can assure you that they *do* talk,' she said. 'They hold long conversations with each other... at least I presume them to be conversations, for I don't understand what they're saying, naturally. When you're as old as I am you'll probably be able to hear them as well; that is, if you retain an open mind about such matters. *Most* people say that as one gets older one believes nothing and is surprised at nothing, so that one becomes more receptive to ideas. Nonsense! All the old people I know have had their minds locked up like grey, scaly oysters since they were in their teens.'

She glanced at me sharply.

'D'you think I'm queer? Touched, eh? Talking about flowers holding conversations?'

Hastily and truthfully I denied this. I said that I thought it was more than likely that flowers conversed with each other. I pointed out that bats produced minute squeaks which I was able to hear, but which would be inaudible to an elderly person, since the sound was too high-pitched.

'That's it, that's it!' she exclaimed delightedly. 'It's a question of wave-length. I put it all down to this slowing-up process. Another thing that you don't notice when you're young is that flowers have personality. They are different from each other, just as people are. Look, I'll show you. D'you see that rose over there, in the bowl by itself?'

On a small table in the corner, enshrined in a small silver bowl, was a magnificent velvety rose, so deep a garnet red that it was almost black. It was a gorgeous flower, the petals curled to perfection, the bloom on them as soft and unblemished as the down on a newly-hatched butterfly's wing.

'Isn't he a beauty?' inquired Mrs. Kralefsky. 'Isn't he wonderful? Now, I've had him two weeks. You'd hardly believe it, would you? And he was not a bud when he came. No, no, he was fully open. But, do you know, he was so sick that I did not think he would live? The person who plucked him was careless enough to put him in with a bunch of Michaelmas daisies.

Fatal, absolutely fatal! You have no idea how cruel the daisy family is, on the whole. They are very rough-and-ready sort of flowers, very down to earth, and, of course, to put such an aristocrat as a rose amongst them is just *asking* for trouble. By the time he got here he had dropped and faded to such an extent that I did not even notice him among the daisies. But, luckily, I heard them at it. I was dozing here when they started, particularly, it seemed to me, the yellow ones, who always seem so belligerent. Well, of course, I didn't know what they were saying, but it sounded *horrible*. I couldn't think *who* they were talking to at first; I thought they were quarrelling among themselves. Then I got out of bed to have a look and I found that poor rose, crushed in the middle of them, being harried to death. I got him out and put him by himself and gave him half an aspirin. Aspirin is so good for roses. Drachma pieces for the chrysanthemums, aspirin for roses, brandy for sweet peas, and a squeeze of lemon-juice for the fleshy flowers, like begonias. Well, removed from the company of the daisies and given that pick-me-up, he revived in no time, and he seems so grateful; he's obviously making an effort to remain beautiful for as long as possible in order to thank me.'

She gazed at the rose affectionately, as it glowed in its silver bowl.

'Yes, there's a lot I have learnt about flowers. They're just like people. Put too many together and they get on each other's nerves and start to wilt. Mix some kinds and you get what appears to be a dreadful form of class distinction. And, of course, the water is so important. Do you know that some people think it's kind to change the water every day? Dreadful! You can hear the flowers dying if you do that. I change the water once a week, put a handful of earth in it, and they thrive.'

GERALD DURRELL

To know how to listen   *To be attentive and silent.*

Flower-Thoughts

Deep spiritual truths, sometimes, become easier to grasp when expressed through simple images. This is a beautiful passage from the Dhammapada, *drawing a series of images, for the seeker, with the help of flowers. It is followed by a short commentary of the Mother on these aphorisms.*

Who will conquer this world of illusion and the kingdom of Yama and the world of the gods? Who will discover the path of the Law as the skilled gardener discovers the rarest of flowers?

The disciple on the right path will conquer this world of illusion and the kingdom of Yama and the world of the gods. He will discover the path of the Law as the skilled gardener discovers the rarest of flowers.

Knowing his body to be as impermanent as foam and as illusory as a mirage, the disciple on the right path will shatter the flowery arrow of Mara and will rise beyond the reach of the King of Death.

Death carries away the man who seeks only the flowers of sensual pleasure just as torrential floods carry away a sleeping village.

Death, the destroyer, overcomes the man who seeks only the flowers of sensual pleasure before he can satisfy himself.

The sage should go from door to door in his village, as the bee gathers honey from the flowers without bringing harm to their colours or their fragrance.

Do not criticise others for what they do or have not done, but be aware of what, yourself, you do or have not done.

Just as a beautiful flower which is radiant yet lacks fragrance, so are the beautiful words of one who does not act accordingly.

Just as a beautiful flower which is both radiant and sweetly scented, so are the beautiful words of one who acts accordingly. Just as many garlands can be made from a heap of flowers, so a mortal can accumulate much merit by good deeds.

The fragrance of flowers, even that of sandalwood or of incense, even that of jasmine, cannot go against the wind; but the sweet fragrance of intelligence goes against the wind. All around the man of intelligence spreads the fragrance of his virtue.

No fragrance, not even that of sandalwood or incense, nor of the lotus nor of jasmine, can be compared with the fragrance of intelligence.

Weak is the fragrance of incense or sandalwood compared to that of a virtuous man which reaches up to the highest of divinities.

Mara cannot discover the way that those beings follow who lead a life of perfect purity and who are liberated by their total knowledge.

As the beautiful scented lily rises by the wayside, even so the disciple of the Perfectly Enlightened One, radiant with intelligence, rises from the blind and ignorant multitude.

THE DHAMMAPADA

There are some very wise recommendations here, for example, not to concern oneself with what others do nor with the mistakes they make, but to attend to one's own faults and negligences and rectify them. Another wise counsel is never to utter too many eloquent words which are not effectuated in action – speak little, act well. Beautiful words, they say, that are mere words, are like flowers without fragrance.

And finally, lest you get discouraged by your own faults, the Dhammapada gives you this solacing image: the purest lily can spring out of a heap of rubbish by the wayside. That is to say, there is nothing so rotten that it cannot give birth to the purest realisation.

Whatever may be the past, whatever may be the faults committed, whatever the ignorance in which one might have lived, one carries deep within oneself the supreme purity which can translate itself into a wonderful realisation.

The whole point is to think of that, to concentrate on that and not to be concerned with all the difficulties and obstacles and hindrances.

Concentrate exclusively on what you want to be, forget as entirely as possible what you do not want to be.

THE MOTHER

A Chinese Flower Diary

It is a great thing when not merely one or a few individuals but an entire people can turn naturally and in joy to flowers. China has been greatly blessed in this regard. Here is a sweet, touching and yet humorous study by Nora Waln.

In Northern Hopeh the time of showers had passed without rain. We had traveled three days over plains, valleys and hills, and seen nothing green except in the irrigated plots near hamlets.

The ancient stone-paved trail led up along a narrow ledge. We waited at the foot for a line of pack coolies to come down. The containers roped on their backs towered high above their heads. Yet, despite his burden, the foremost man swerved out suddenly to the edge of the cliff and, as they came on, all of the men behind him did the same.

When they had passed us, we began our climb. My pack coolie was before me. When I came up to the place round which the others had swerved, he was pouring the last contents of his canteen into a crevice. There, through the dust between the stones, a wild rose had grown – a perfect flower, beautifully tinted and sweetly fragrant. "It is from such a one as this," my coolie said, "that we learn fortitude."

It was in the province of Kwangtung. The temple was dirty and neglected. I chided the abbot concerning the dust on a Buddha's face. He did not answer me immediately. He led me along a dark narrow passage, opened a door and motioned to me to go through it. Beyond I stood in a tiny garden above a deep ravine. No weeds grew in the rich, much-worked loam. A low wall of carefully placed rocks kept the garden from sliding down the mountainside.

In his garden, the abbot spoke: "The furniture on an altar is but the symbol of religion… in the face of a flower the heart of God is revealed."

I had no answer. At my feet were tall white lilies, each with a golden heart. Over my head a magnolia was in bloom.

Lifting a clump of pansies with a careful trowel, the abbot planted them in an earthen pot. "Take this home," he said. "If you are one who sincerely seeks the truth, by living with a flower you will find it."

Bald-The-Third, my serving matron, was stiff with anger. A filthy beggar had erected a mat shed against the wall of our residence at Nanking, and settled down to live by the gate which led from our garden to the hill path. He would have to go, she declared. Disease would be carried over the wall by every breeze. Probably Small Girl would die of cholera.

Bald-The-Third went out to clear him away. Later I discovered her seated on the sewing-room floor hemstitching a sheet, an occupation she used to calm herself when she has been overwrought.

"Has the beggar gone?" I asked.

"No – he is still there," she answered.

"Oh! He defeated you in argument?" I pressed her.

"I did not speak to him," she said. "He has a sprig of jasmine growing in a broken pot and has given it the least drafty place in his miserable shelter. He hadn't much tea, but he was sharing what he had with the flower. I do not think such a man will do us harm. People can be too concerned regarding physical health and neglect the health of the spirit. I've sent him out a gift of rice and fish."

The Chinese love of flowers has been re-

warded by genius in their cultivation. Flowers are coddled, nursed and coaxed. There is a vast lore of wisdom passed orally from generation to generation concerning the whims and peculiarities of different plants – also a voluminous detailed gardening literature in which the observations of centuries are garnered. In the House of Exile library there are 40 books, considered classics, on the culture of chrysanthemums only, and nearly as many relating to dwarf trees.

Chinese people do not like to cut their flowers, and seldom do. The flowers displayed at a festival are growing, either in pots or in the ground.

In heat, plants are sheltered in the coolest places in the homestead, and shades are erected for blossoming trees, vines and flowers. I have seen people sit all through the breathless tropic noon fanning a drooping flower. In cold, plants are housed in paper shelters, their roots set in loam warmed by subterranean air pipes heated by buried charcoal.

These are constructed today exactly as decreed by a ruler of Wei who lived more than 2,000 years ago. He ordered that they should be so simply designed that even the poorest and most stupid of his people might make one. In the most severe weather, florists clothe buds in little paper coats perforated with breathing holes.

Although they perform an infinite amount of toil in bringing their flowers to perfection, florists charge astonishingly low prices. A florist once told me that a country in which flowers – necessity for the refinement of the heart – were priced so as to make them a luxury was a country which had yet to learn the first principles of civilization.

I had lost my way and had to ask a policeman for direction. I drew my car up to the curb and waited. The policeman was occupied. Using his teapot as a watering can, he was watering the phlox which he had placed around his stance on the modern concrete road.

When he had finished, he gave me the information I required. But before he signalled me to move on he said: "There is no day in the year when flowers fail to bless China with their lovely charm. Is this also so in the Outer World?"

NORA WALN

Green Fingers

Some have green fingers…their gardens will thrive –
In every weather their plants will survive.
Soil may be poor and the air may be cold –
Yet 'neath green fingers – bulbs shoot and unfold –
Defying the foes that attack other flowers –
Seeming to grow with miraculous powers…
Blight cannot touch them and pests cannot harm –
held in the spell of some magical charm.
What is the reason? Does anyone know –
Why one will die and the other will grow.
…Flowers have their feelings: Yes – Flowers understand –
if there is love in the touch of a hand.

Flower-Haikus

In Japan the love of flowers has reached a completely unique dimension – unimaginable for persons not tuned to that way of seeing and feeling. A few of its very typical manifestations can be seen in Haiku-poems and the art of flower arrangement.

One Haiku relates that a girl went out early one morning to draw water from the village well. But during the night a Morning-glory had wound itself round the rope on which the bucket hung, and put forth a single blossom which opened its face to the light of day, drunk with joy. The girl, delighted and disconcerted at once, could not bring herself to disturb this wonderful happening. From a more distant well she filled her buckets and carried them back with a joyful heart, paying no heed to the long detour.

The poem by Chiyo-ni says:
   Lend me water please?
   Some fresh young
   Morning-glory
   Careless…took my well.

Here are some more Haikus on flowers each commemorating a different perception or experience.

> In the city field
>   Contemplating
>   Cherry-trees…
> Strangers are like friends

Issa

> My two plum trees are
>   So gracious…
>   See, they flower
> One now, one later

Buson

For a lovely bowl
    Let us arrange these
      Flowers…
Since there is no rice

            BASHO

    In the endless rain
      Is it turning
        Sunward still…
    Trusting hollyhock?

            BASHO

That white peony…
    Lover of the moon
      Trembling
Now at twilight

            GYODAI

    A short summer night…
      But in this solemn
        Darkness
    One peony bloomed

            BUSON

One fallen flower
    Returning to the
    Branch?…Oh no!
A white butterfly

            MORITAKE

Camellia-petal
Fell in silent dawn…
Spilling
A water-jewel

            BASHO

White chrysanthemums
    Making all else
    About them
Reflected riches

            CHORA

Too curious flower
      Watching us pass,
      Met death…
Our hungry donkey

            BASHO

Zen in Flower Arrangement

Look at a vase full of beautiful flowers. Is it not a small part of Nature brought into the house, creating a silent sanctuary where meet man and his Creator?

In Japan the art of flower arrangement surpasses all conventional ideas of art. The aim, it is said, is to achieve a state of 'artless art'. It is meditation, it is self-finding and self-expression. It is a way of life. It is a treading of the flower way. These excerpts are from the revealing book, 'Zen in the Art of Flower arrangement', by Justin L. Herrigel.

Art is studied in Japan not only for art's sake, but for spiritual enlightenment. If art stops short at art and does not lead to something deeper and more fundamental, if, that is to say, art does not become equivalent to something spiritual, the Japanese would not consider it worth learning. Art and religion are closely bound up with one another in the history of Japanese culture. The art of flower arrangement is not, in its truest sense, an art, but rather the expression of a much deeper experience of life. The flowers should be arranged in such a way that we are reminded of the lilies of the field, whose beauty was not surpassed by Solomon in all his glory. Even the modest wild flower, named nazuma, was regarded with reverence by Basho, the Japanese haiku poet of the seventeenth century. For it proclaims the deeper secret of Nature, which is an 'artless art'.

*

The summons to mindfulness is more important than zealous enthusiasm. Nor is it sufficient to set about one's work as though one were going to five o'clock tea. Arranging flowers is no pastime and is not intended for distraction. You must collect yourself beforehand and begin early in the morning by performing all your activities without fuss, without haste, and giving them the expression of inner balance and harmony. This attitude should become so natural that it turns into a secure possession. One can well say that the 'inner work' of flower arrangement must keep pace with the outer. Only so can it be a wholeness of heaven, man, and earth. The hour for arranging the flowers pervades the entire day, it does not stand outside. But it is not easy to go the modest way of the flowers from morning till evening!

*

In a book of rules for memorizing, the rudiments of the inner and outer attitude required for arranging flowers are laid down:

Behave well in class and do not chatter. It is unbecoming to behave as though one knew more than one does in reality, far better to act modestly.

Be proud of nothing; there are stages beyond the one you are on now.

If anyone is outwardly skilled in flower arrangement, yet lacks artistic and human delicacy of feeling, he is nevertheless ignorant.

Whoever, through his way of arranging flowers, can make a room beautiful with harmony and good taste, is to be called skilful, even if his way of arranging them is unskilful.

It is deemed a politeness not to execute any hasty movements.

Flowers should be handled tenderly.

Do not expect more from the flowers than their nature can bear.

Do not look down on other schools, but take from them whatever is good. Drop anything bad, even if it comes from your own school.

Superficiality always leads to perversity.

*

An old tradition lists the ten virtues which the Flower-Master must make his own if he wants to penetrate into the spirit of the 'true teaching', and which he at the same time acquires once he has penetrated into it. In quite simple words something is said that at first sight looks insignificant, indeed childish. But here, as so often in the Far East, one must know how to read between the lines.

1. Flower-setting brings high and low into spiritual relationship.
2. Carry 'Nothing' in the heart. It is 'Everything'.
3. Quiet, clear feeling. You can reach solutions without thinking.
4. Freedom from all cares.
5. Intimate, sensitive relationships with plants and the essence of Nature.
6. Love and esteem all men.
7. Fill the room with harmony and reverence.
8. 'True spirit' nourishes life; combine flower arrangement with religious feeling.
9. Harmony of body and soul.
10. Self-denial and reserve; freedom from evil.

*

All this emphasizes the connexion and reciprocal action between men, plants and the world. If, therefore, the pupil treads the 'flowers' way aright, it will be clear to him from the beginning that the way does not lead into separate tracks. He is not guided only into outward, concrete, visible activity, for only silent communion with himself leaves him peaceful, relaxed, and devout enough to pass on to his work. From the centre of his being, from his inner self-collection, the way leads in a straight, harmonious line to the outer world. His eyes are filled with the wonder and beauty of the plants lying before him. Joined to the all-uniting being, taken up into the whole of the cosmos, he can create from the centre of his own humanity.

It may be that the pupil will look at the meaning of his task from two sides at first, until he is able to bring it to uniform expression. On the one hand he will develop quietness, patience and perseverance in his work. On the other, he will try to introduce as much as possible

of this way of working into his practical life. Thus he does not stand still on the path, but can develop manysidedly and find the middle way. He has given the flowers a new, living form and composition, and – without willing it – has put this form outside himself and inside himself simultaneously. This mutual interaction in the sense of the original teaching has seized his whole being, filled it, rounded it out. He lives in harmonious union with himself, his surroundings, and the universe. He is sustained by heaven as well as by the earth. And the natural way leads still further, beyond the symbolic handling of the flowers, the spouting water, the form-giving rocks. The pupil goes the 'flowers' way not only in the isolated hour of practice or ceremonial. The living, creative presence of these hours will accompany him and lead him onward. The way can accompany life itself with ever new prospects and new beginnings. From this standpoint one can understand the saying that one treads this way 'as if not treading it', which means that way and pupil have become one.

*

It should be evident from what has been said that flower arrangement is concerned with this inner, spiritual principle. But one must be quite clear that the right attitude has nothing to do with mood. That which underlies this art and needs to be experienced is in itself formless, but it takes on form as soon as you try to represent it symbolically. And it is just this spiritual form that constitutes the essence of flower arrangement. By adhering strictly to the cosmic pattern, the artist learns, in accordance with the Eastern attitude of pure, unpurposing surrender to the laws of the cosmos, to experience them through and through. At the same time he breaks through to the depths of his own being, which rests on those same laws.

Here without doubt is the key to an understanding of Eastern art and the spiritual life of the East in general: in this 'looking away from oneself', in the utter 'unpurposingness' of its highest spiritual achievements. Thus the painter brushes his strokes not as though *he* painted them, but as though they painted themselves from the primal 'Ground'. Thus, too, the flowers are not brought into harmony by looking at them first from one side and then from the other, by experimenting and comparing – only the beginner does that – rather, the eye is directed inwards. Not the slightest intention of arranging them 'beautifully' must disturb this self-immersion, not even the desire to become 'purposeless on purpose'. If you succeed in producing this frame of mind and in keeping it pure, then only does the hand unconsciously follow spontaneous impulses. This attitude only *looks* passive; according to the Eastern view, it is in reality the source of that inner strength.

Stages of Knowledge

It goes without saying that there are stages along the 'flowers' way which the Master can recognize and knows how to interpret. He shows the pupil the degree of knowledge he has now attained. Often he can read the beginner's character with uncanny accuracy from the way he arranges his flowers and does his work.

Spontaneity and individuality seldom appear during the initial stages. Only through patient practice and continual inner transformation does habit gradually wear away, until the work manifests the 'pure form'. At highest stages of development the pupil's 'originality' can venture forth more freely, till finally it becomes more and more purified and blends with the 'pure truth' in the perfect unity of art and nature.

Thus the 'truth' finds, in the essential nature of the artist, the theatre in which it takes on visible form. To embody the truth of 'Heaven itself' – this is the highest task, whose solution is granted only to the best poets and painters. And if he is successful, the flower artist will find it rising out of himself with unforced naturalness, like a gift that can never be lost.

Yet behind the visible forms there is always the form that cannot be expressed and cannot be represented, the eternal mystery, which he struggles in vain to apprehend, unless it reveal itself unhoped for.

*

In spite of its delicacy, flower arrangement was originally practised by men, more particularly by those well tested by life. Self-immersion in union with the flowers breathes the very spirit of the samurai, and the gravity of final, irrevocable decisions.

Imagine what tremendous inner strength is expressed when the lord of a castle, which has already surrendered to the superior assaults of the enemy, still remains calm and composed enough to arrange flowers! This act may well be the last he will ever do, but it is not one of violence. It does not pretend to be anything special, it simply bears the stamp of something involuntary, of a true and detached life, of an art that is just as unartificial as the practice of 'true' archery.

Not only outwardly is the lord of the castle a knight, inwardly too he remains a victor not to be conquered by his foe. He is as unshakable in the face of death as he was in life. His being flows from the centre, which carries both heaven and earth, and is carried by both.

JUSTIN L. HERRIGEL

The true consciousness is that you do the right thing not because it is your duty to do it, not because it is worthy to do it and it is expected of you to do it, but because your nature impels you towards it. The flower blooms spontaneously without any sense of duty. It possesses no sense of duty because its nature is to do so, to be beautiful. Human beings also could be like that, spontaneous and natural in its action and behaviour. When you do a great thing, you do not feel that you are doing something marvellous or that you are exercising or stretching your power. You do not do a thing because it is your duty to do it but because it is your nature to do so, you cannot but do it.

NOLINI KANTA GUPTA

Acknowledgements

Our grateful thanks to the following:

For the excerpts from their Publications

- Sri Aurobindo Ashram Trust for the writings of Sri Aurobindo and the Mother
- *White Roses* (Copyright Huta)
- Atlantis Harvest '*A Chinese Flower Diary*' by Nora Waln
- Flammarion – Paris '*My Family and other Animals*' by Gerald Durrell
- Peter Pauper Press, New York, '*Japanese Haiku*'; '*The Four Seasons*'
- Routledge & Kegan Paul, London, '*Zen in the Art of Flower Arrangement*' by Justin L. Herrigel

For the Photographs

- Sri Aurobindo Ashram Trust for the photographs of the Mother
- Achim Brockhaus
- Ashatit Poddar
- Elizabeth Beck
- Indra Poddar
- Kanak Ganguly
- Nirmal Jhunjhunwala
- Sudha Sundaram
- Vidyavrata

For the Paintings

- Chanda Poddar
- Mahesh Poddar
- Sushanto

4